Learning to learn for life

Rebecca Goodbourn

Steve Higgins

Susie Parsons

Kate Wall

and Julia Wright

research and practical examples for the
Foundation Stage and Key Stage 1

CAMPAIGN FOR **LEARNING**

CAMPAIGN
FOR **LEARNING**

Published by Network Educational Press Ltd
PO Box 635
Stafford
ST16 1BF

© Campaign for Learning 2005

ISBN 1 85539 178 3

Managing editor: Janice Baiton – Janice Baiton Editorial Services
Design and typesetting: Neil Hawkins – Network Educational Press

Printed by MPG Books Ltd, Bodmin, Cornwall

Contents

Contributing authors 4

Acknowledgements 5

Foreword

Stephen Twigg, MP, Minister of State for School Standards 8
Department for Education and Skills

Introduction 9

Section One 11
Learning to learn for life

Section Two 15
The Learning to Learn in Schools Action Research Project

Section Three 33
Practical experience of learning to learn – case studies from the Foundation Stage
and Key Stage 1

1 Introducing the Personal Effectiveness Programme Initiative (PEPI) 35
   into an infant school
   Janet Thomas and Laurel Barber, Hazelbury Infant School

2 Stop! Time to reflect 51
   Shelley Long and Lindsey Weedall, Leaf Lane Infant and Nursery School

3 The role of the environment in developing lifelong learners 63
   Nicola Furnish and Helen Tonkin, Pennoweth Community Primary School

4 Does introducing parents to learning to learn techniques have a 75
   positive effect on pupils' achievement?
   Linda Stephens, St Meriadoc Church of England Nursery and Infant School

5 Implementing and developing 'learning mats' and 'stuck mats' in Key Stage 1 87
   Fleur McAlvey and Mary Barrett, St Saviours Catholic Infant School

6 The impact of formative assessment strategies on behaviour, self-esteem 95
   and attainment
   Ann Webb, Treloweth Community Primary School

7 Using formative assessment strategies to improve children's writing or 105
   'Nobody's brain is ever full up!'
   Ann Mulcahy and Elaine Saini, Wilbury Primary School

Section Four 115
Developing learning to learn in your school

Section Five 123
Useful resources

Index 126

Contributing authors

Janet Thomas and Laurel Barber, Hazelbury Infant School, Enfield

Shelley Long and Lindsey Weedall, Leaf Lane Infant and Nursery School, Cheshire

Nicola Furnish and Helen Tonkin, Pennoweth Community Primary School, Cornwall

Linda Stephens, St Meriadoc Church of England Nursery and Infant School, Cornwall

Fleur McAlvey and Mary Barrett, St Saviours Catholic Infant School, Cheshire

Ann Webb, Treloweth Cummunity Primary School, Cornwall

Ann Mulcahy and Elaine Saini, Wilbury Primary School, Enfield

Acknowledgements

This book would not have been written without the help and support of many people and organizations, most importantly the schools taking part in Phase 3 of our Learning to Learn Action Research Project and their teachers and pupils whose hard work and dedication is the foundation of the book.

From Cheshire Local Education Authority

- Brereton Church of England Primary School
- Fallibroome High School
- Henbury High School
- Holmes Chapel Primary School
- John Street Primary School
- Leaf Lane Infant and Nursery School
- Over Hall Community School
- St Saviours Catholic Infant School
- Sutton High School
- Winsford High Street Primary School
- Wolverham Primary School
- Woodford Lodge High School

From Cornwall Local Education Authority and Education Action Zone

- Alverton Primary School
- Brannel School
- Camborne Science and Community College
- Kehelland Village School
- Lanner Primary School
- Mounts Bay Secondary School
- Pennoweth Community Primary School
- Pool School and Community College
- The Roseland Community School
- St Meriadoc Church of England Nursery and Infant School
- Treloweth Community Primary School

From the London Borough of Enfield Local Education Authority and Edmonton Education Action Zone

- Aylward School

- Brettenham Primary School

- Fleecefield Primary School

- Hazelbury Infant School

- Hazelbury Junior School

- Oakthorpe Primary School

- Raynham Primary School

- Wilbury Primary School

We would also like to thank the following people and organizations.

The Project Advisory Board, which is chaired by Susie Parsons with the secretariat provided by Rebecca Goodbourn, and whose members are:

Jackie Beere, Campion School
Benoit Charles, London Borough of Enfield
Professor Guy Claxton, Bristol University
Sheila Dainton, Association of Teachers and Lecturers
Maggie Farrar, National College of School Leadership
Mike Gibbons, Innovation Unit, Department for Education and Skills
Toby Greany, Design Council
Paul Hanbury, Cornwall County Council
John Hattersley, Cheshire County Council
Oona Hickie, ICT in Schools Division, Department for Education and Skills
Steve Higgins, University of Newcastle
Dr Peter Honey, Peter Honey Publications and Patron of the Campaign for Learning
Jim Houghton, Network Educational Press
Chris Hughes, Ofsted
Naz Khan, London Borough of Enfield
Dr David Leat, University of Newcastle
Dr Bill Lucas, Patron of the Campaign for Learning
Jenny Mosley, Jenny Mosley Consultancies
Tim Oates, QCA
Stephen Rogers, University of the First Age
Colin Rose, Accelerated Learning Systems
Sue Sayer, Cornwall County Council
Professor Judy Sebba, University of Sussex
Carol Singh, National Primary Strategy
Alistair Smith, Alite Ltd
Steve Strand, nferNelson
Kate Wall, University of Newcastle
Professor Sheila Wolfendale, University of East London
Julia Wright, Campaign for Learning.

Our research partner: The Centre for Learning and Teaching at the University of Newcastle, particularly the project leaders Steve Higgins and Kate Wall and their colleagues Chris Falzon, Elaine Hall, David Leat, Viv Baumfield, Jill Clark, Gail Edwards, Hanneke Jones, Lisa Murtagh, Fay Smith and Pam Woolner.

Our major sponsors: the Innovation Unit and the ICT in Schools Division of the DfES, the National College for School Leadership and nferNelson.

All the other organizations which have supported us along the way and of course our publishers, Network Educational Press.

Any accidental errors or omissions are the responsibility of the Campaign for Learning.

Foreword

Helping children to develop as confident, enthusiastic and effective learners is a central purpose of primary education. One of the most important things we can do in schools is to provide a range of learning opportunities that will enable this to happen. I am therefore delighted to have been asked to provide the foreword to the Campaign for Learning's publication *Learning to learn for life*.

The research and resources that follow will, I believe, complement the work of the Primary National Strategy and in particular the Teaching and Learning materials recently introduced. A key feature of our teaching and learning materials is the discussion and promotion of aspects of learning and this is something that comes through very strongly in this publication.

The findings of this research also confirm the value of using 'learning to learn' approaches as part of the effort to personalize learning and the importance of planning learning and development activities for children based on observation of their progress. This evidence base demonstrates that by using and adapting a range of methods, schools and teachers can satisfy the learning needs of individual children. In doing this, they can ensure that learning is right for each child at each stage of their development, stimulating them to become more confident, self-aware, independent and effective learners.

Finally, I wanted to say how exciting it is to see how the schools involved in the Learning to Learn Action Research Project are exploring how technologies can support and enhance the learning process. We are keen to encourage better use of ICT to improve learning, including catering for different learning styles. These resources will help achieve that.

Stephen Twigg, MP
Minister of State for School Standards
Department for Education and Skills

Introduction

Following on from our previous publications, *Teaching pupils how to learn* and *Creating a learning to learn school*, which span both primary and secondary education, this is the first book in our Learning to Learn for Life series of research and practical examples and ideas for everyone interested in developing better schools and lifelong learners. This book has a particular emphasis on the Foundation Stage and Key Stage 1. The other key stages will feature in later publications.

The Campaign for Learning believes that the teacher's voice must be heard loud and clear in any discussion of improvements in education. Teachers are the people who are best placed to tell us what works and what does not. For this reason, the Learning to Learn in Schools Action Research Project is led by the teachers involved in the project, who have selected and developed their own interventions in their schools. We are very grateful to those who have contributed their experience to this book.

The book is separated into five clear sections:

Section One outlines what learning to learn is.

Section Two outlines what the Learning to Learn in Schools Action Research Project is, what it is trying to achieve and the results so far.

Section Three focuses on case studies and actual activities that you can adapt for your school.

Section Four aims to help you move learning to learn forward in your school.

Section Five provides a list of helpful resources.

Related publications

- *Learning to learn: setting an agenda for schools in the 21st century* (Bill Lucas and Toby Greany; Campaign for Learning, Network Educational Press, 2001) sets out the original thinking behind the project.

- *Teaching pupils how to learn: research, practice and INSET resources* (Bill Lucas, Toby Greany, Jill Rodd and Ray Wicks; Campaign for Learning, Network Educational Press, 2002) sets out the findings from Phase 1 of the research and is aimed at a general teaching audience.

- *Creating a learning to learn school: research and practice for raising standards, motivation and morale* (Toby Greany and Jill Rodd; Campaign for Learning, Network Educational Press, 2003) sets out the findings from Phase 2 of the research and is aimed at a general teaching audience.

- Separate research reports by Jill Rodd covering Phases 1 and 2 are available from the Campaign's website www.campaignforlearning.org.uk.

- Research report by Steve Higgins, Kate Wall, et al. covering year one of Phase 3 of the project is available from the Campaign's website www.campaignforlearning.org.uk.

Asking the pupils

Every two years the Campaign runs a MORI questionnaire to track secondary school student views of schools and the way they learn. While this book is aimed at teachers working in the Foundation Stage and Key Stage 1, their pupils will go on to secondary schools. What will their experience be?

Depressingly, as the table below shows, copying from a board or a book is still what secondary school students say they do most often and learning things that relate to the real world is mentioned least often. The Learning to Learn in Schools Action Research Project aims to change this!

Which three of the following do you do most often in class?

	2000 (%)	2002 (%)	2004 (%)
Copy from the board or a book	56	63	61
Have a class discussion	37	31	32
Listen to a teacher talking for a long time	37	37	39
Take notes while my teacher talks	26	20	20
Work in small groups to solve a problem	25	22	23
Spend time thinking quietly on my own	22	24	24
Talk about my work with a teacher	22	16	18
Work on a computer	12	10	20
Learn things that relate to the real world	11	12	14

We are very grateful to Select Education for sponsoring our MORI poll.

Source: MORI Omnibus survey, 2000, 2002, 2004

Section One

Learning to learn for life

> *If, during our school years, we could not merely learn a specific content but could also learn how the process of learning itself works and can be improved, then we would be better equipped for all later learning.*

Professor David Hargreaves (2004)

We live in an uncertain world where we do not know what we will need to learn in the future. Technological advances are rapid. The internet gives us ready access to a mass of undifferentiated information, so everyone needs to be able to select, evaluate and process information and to discard what is not needed or helpful. Today, people are less likely to stay in the same job for life. They may change jobs within an industry or move between industries and sectors. Even if they do stay in the same organization, jobs and roles can change dramatically during a working life. Changes in the economy and in technology have meant that the types of jobs that people are doing have changed. Britain is no longer predominantly a manufacturing economy but increasingly a service and knowledge-based economy. In the past, a large number of jobs did not require basic literacy skills, while today the vast majority involve intermediate or advanced level skills and the Director-General of the CBI, Digby Jones, predicts that in a few years' time anyone who is without a skill will be without a job.

Since we do not know what people will need to learn in the future, it makes sense to develop confident, successful lifelong learners who are ready to learn anything, able to cope with uncertainty and skilled at managing and processing knowledge. Many people talk of lifelong learning as what happens to some of us after we leave compulsory education at the age of 16. In fact, of course, lifelong learning means just that – learning from cradle to grave. We are well-programmed to learn from the outset. As babies, we learn to walk and talk and explore the world without really being aware that we are learning. Once we enter the formal education system, we are taught reading, writing and using numbers, often with an emphasis on *what* we are learning rather than *how* we learn. The main function of formal education should be to help people to learn – to give them the motivation and the ability to be confident successful learners as well as focusing on the content of their learning. This is not to suggest that content is unimportant, quite the contrary. Content and process are inextricably linked. You cannot develop thinking skills without something interesting to think about.

The Campaign for Learning defines 'learning to learn' as a process of discovery about learning. It involves a set of principles and skills that, if understood and used, help learners learn more effectively and so become learners for life. At its heart is the belief that learning is learnable.

Learning to learn is essentially about the process of learning. It offers pupils: an awareness of how they prefer to learn and their learning strengths; how they can motivate themselves and have the self-confidence to succeed; factors they should consider, such as the importance of hydration, nutrition, sleep and a positive environment for learning; some specific strategies they can use, such as improving their memory or making sense of complex information; and some habits they should develop, such as reflecting on their learning so as to improve next time.

A positive aspect was being treated more like adults and having the responsibility.

Pupil, Lanner Primary School, Cornwall

For teachers, learning to learn is about wanting more for your students and involving them in their own learning process.

Children respond positively if they are included and consulted about the learning process. They have very clear ideas about what they think should happen. It is useful for a teacher to know what these thoughts are even if they choose not to do anything about them.

Teacher, John Street Primary, Cheshire

In *Teaching Children to Learn*, Professor Guy Claxton (2004) argues that there have been three generations of teaching learning, each one more powerful than the rest and each one overlapping and lingering, and that the third generation is rapidly metamorphosing into the fourth. The fourth generation will be characterized, among other things, by greater intellectual rigour, more engagement of students in how to build learning power, whole-school learning to learn strategies, more involvement of parents and the wider community and more focus on learning for life.

First Generation ⬇	Raising attainment Outcome of schooling (e.g. KS2 SATs results) Good teaching was about content and acquisition Good teachers could put across information, develop literacy and numeracy, and so on
Second Generation ⬇	Develop study skills Hints and tips on retaining and recalling for tests Practising techniques Good teaching as before, plus delivering above techniques
Third Generation ⬇	Expanded to include emotional factors (e.g. self-esteem) Characteristic ways of learning (e.g. multiple intelligences) Good teaching included reducing stress levels and helping students raise their attainment levels Concerned with the 'how' of teaching
Fourth Generation	Involvement of students in the processes Concerned with 'how' students can be helped to help themselves (e.g. think creatively) Teachers themselves involved in becoming better learners Developmental and cumulative – encouraging the 'ready and willing', not just the 'able'

Teaching learning – the four generations, Professor Guy Claxton (2004)

> *Finally, perhaps the most profound shift from G3 to the fourth generation is the real commitment to helping students develop habits, values, skills and dispositions that will be of use to them in 'the big wide world' as well as in the context of school attainment. G3 approaches had the rhetoric of lifelong learning but tended, in practice, to slide back into focusing on traditional, more familiar, priorities. Now there is a new resolve to see education as a preparation for a learning life.*

Professor Guy Claxton (2004)

The present government has placed great emphasis on and pumped considerable resources into improving education, and learning to learn is increasingly being recognized as central to this drive (DfES, 2004a). As the then Minister for School Standards, David Miliband, made clear at the Campaign for Learning's 2004 Learning to Learn Conference:

> *The answer to how to move towards a high-quality, high-equity education system lies in the schools. What is needed is personalized learning, tailored to the needs, interests and aptitudes of each individual pupil. The relevance of this conference today is immediately clear. Good teachers are critical but our biggest untapped resource is the energies of students. This goes to the heart of what the Campaign for Learning and personalized learning is all about. The ideas and insights from the Campaign for Learning fit squarely within personalized learning and should be central to the way in which we take it forward. I hope that from this conference you will create a professional learning community to drive learning to learn forward. I am pleased that my Department is supporting the Campaign in this.*

In 2003 the Department for Education and Skills (DfES) published *Excellence and Enjoyment: A strategy for primary schools*, which urged teachers to develop the distinctive character of their schools, to take ownership of the curriculum and to be creative and innovative in how they teach and run a school. Since the publication of the primary strategy, the DfES has produced the *Excellence and Enjoyment: Learning and teaching in the primary years* professional development materials (2004b), which encompass learning to learn ideas. The materials are structured around three key themes with two units for each theme. These are:

Planning and assessment for learning
Designing opportunities for learning
Assessment for learning

Creating a learning culture
The conditions for learning
Classroom community, collaborative and personalized learning

Understanding how learning develops
Learning to learn: progression in key aspects of learning
Learning to learn: key aspects of learning across the curriculum

The materials are available from the DfES website www.standards.dfes.gov.uk/primary/publications.

Thinking about learning to learn is developing all the time. Projects such as ELLI (The Effective Learning Power Profile), Learning How to Learn: in Classrooms, Schools and Networks (see boxes overleaf) and the Campaign for Learning's Action Research Project (described in the next section) are providing new insights into teaching that supports learning. The teachers, pupils and students taking part in such projects are at the forefront of this development.

The ELLI (Effective Learning Power Profile) project

The ELLI project has been co-ordinated by Professor Patricia Broadfoot, Professor Guy Claxton and Dr Ruth Deakin Crick at Bristol University's Graduate School of Education. The project identified seven underlying dimensions to 'Learning Power' from a study that included over 1,600 learners from the age of 7 to 25. These dimensions represent the ways in which learners are energized to think, feel and behave in learning situations. The seven dimensions are:

- Growth orientation – a commitment to growth and change over time
- Meaning making – the capacity to make personally meaningful connections
- Critical curiosity – the tendency to want to get below the surface and find things out
- Creativity – the capacity to use imagination, playfulness and intuition
- Learning relationships – being able to learn with and from other people
- Strategic awareness – the capacity to be aware of how learning is happening
- Dependence and fragility – the contrast to all the positive dimensions.

The Effective Learning Power Profile includes a range of assessment tools that can be used to track and develop these aspects of Learning Power. The ELLI project has involved working with a group of schools (including one of the Learning to Learn project schools) to explore how the Learning Power dimensions could be developed within the classroom.

Sixteen teachers used the Effective Learning Power Profiles with their classes to identify which aspects of Learning Power they would focus on developing. They then integrated the chosen Learning Power Dimensions into their learning objectives and after two terms the children were assessed again to see if their Learning Power Profile had changed. The classes showed significant increases on the positive Learning Power Dimensions and had also reduced their profiles on fragility and dependence. However, in control classes matched to the experimental group where there were no Learning Power interventions the Learning Power Profile actually decreased over the course of the year.

Key text: *Building Learning Power*, Guy Claxton (2002)

The Learning How to Learn in Classrooms, Schools and Networks project

The Learning How to Learn project has been co-ordinated by Dr Mary James (University of Cambridge), Professor Robert McCormick (Open University) and Professor Dylan Wiliam (King's College London) and is a Teaching and Learning Research Programme project. The hypothesis of the project is that *Teachers and schools need to develop the processes and practices of learning how to learn if they are to create the conditions for pupils to learn and to learn how to learn.*

The four-year project involves four universities (Cambridge, Reading, The Open University and King's College, London) working in partnership with schools in five LEAs (Oxford, Medway, Hertfordshire, Redbridge and Essex) and two Virtual Education Action Zones.

The research and development project aims to advance both understanding and practice of learning how to learn in classrooms, schools and networks. More specifically it will:

- develop 'assessment for learning' into a model of learning how to learn for both teachers and pupils;
- investigate what teachers can do to help pupils to learn how to learn;
- investigate what characterizes the school in which teachers successfully create and manage the knowledge and skills of learning how to learn;
- investigate how educational networks can support the creation, management and transfer of the knowledge and skills of learning how to learn;
- attempt to develop a generic model of innovation in teaching and learning that integrates work in classrooms, schools and networks.

www.learntolearn.ac.uk

Section Two

The Learning to Learn in Schools Action Research Project

Phase 1	2000 – 2001	Action research in 24 schools across England and Wales	Research published 2002
			Teaching pupils how to learn
Phase 2	2001 – 2002	Action research in 16 schools across England and Wales	Research published 2003
			Creating a learning to learn school
Phase 3	2003 – 2007	Action research in 32 schools in Cheshire Cornwall Enfield	Year 1 research published 2005 *Learning to learn for life: research and practical examples for the foundation stage and key stage 1*
			Year 2 report to be published 2006
			Year 3 report to be published 2007

The Campaign for Learning is an independent charity which aims to stimulate learning that will sustain people for life. It focuses on three main areas: learning at work, family and community learning, and learning in school. It runs national awareness-raising events, including Learning at Work Day and Family Learning Week, and works in a range of ways to change policy and practice on learning. The Campaign is working for an inclusive society in which learning is understood, valued and accessible to everyone as of right. Visit www.campaignforlearning.org.uk for more details.

Much of the Campaign's activity in workplaces and in families and communities is directed towards helping people who are disengaged from learning to switch back on. Our work in schools aims to assist teachers to make sure that their pupils stay switched on – building on the enthusiasm for learning that everyone is born with and that is evident to anyone watching a small child exploring the world. The rationale for the Learning to Learn in Schools project is to understand how we can help pupils learn most effectively and so give each one the best chance to achieve his or her full potential. In practice, this entails investigating a range of interventions aimed at recognizing and supporting pupils' different learning styles and at making the learning process more explicit so as to develop independent learning skills and boost motivation. The project also investigates the impact of learning how to learn on pupil attainment and on teacher morale.

What is Action Research?

The Learning to Learn project uses a teacher-led professional enquiry approach, also known as action research. This is:

● research by individuals on their own work;

● carried out by teachers who want to introduce change and to evaluate the impact of this change;

● about asking questions and hypothesizing – not just about trying to find solutions to existing problems;

● systematic and planned;

● most successful if it is collaborative;

● most likely to succeed if supported with the expertise of research assistants and tutors from other agencies, such as universities;

● based on the collection of evidence and reflection on the evidence and the process;

● about the critical analysis and systematic questioning of existing practice in order to effect desirable changes in the classroom.

Phases 1 and 2

In September 2000 the Campaign for Learning launched a two-year Action Research Project involving 24 schools with pupils aged 3 to 16 years old. The research aimed to understand the impact of teachers and schools adopting learning to learn approaches in terms of pupil achievement and wider learning.

The participating schools were involved in developing the overall project definition and framework for learning to learn, which was expressed as a mind map.

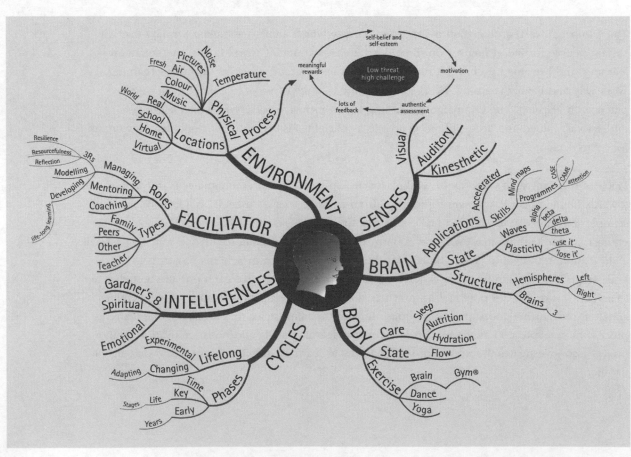

The schools then defined their own areas of interest and developed research hypotheses and approaches in discussion with the Campaign for Learning's research leader, Dr Jill Rodd. All the schools collected a range of qualitative and quantitative data and the majority identified target and comparison groups. The schools adopted a variety of approaches to implementing learning to learn, ranging from timetabled learning to learn induction courses for pupils in Year 7, to courses for parents in how they can best support their children's learning, to whole-school strategies exploring different aspects of effective learning environments and teaching approaches

There are some limitations to an action research approach. Principal among these is the difficulty of generalizing from findings from 24 different schools and the lack of comparability. In order to overcome this the project adopted a case study-based approach, with contextual variables explored through cross-case analysis.

Based on this approach, the research suggested that learning to learn approaches can help:

- raise standards
- boost pupil motivation and confidence in learning
- enhance teacher motivation and morale.

Phases 1 and 2 of the Learning to Learn project were extremely successful in providing initial research evidence for the impact of a number of learning to learn approaches already widely in use in schools and in systematizing what is known, developing a common language and exploring and publicizing approaches that teachers have found to work well. For the teachers involved, the project also provided an opportunity for professional development, with many gaining promotion, becoming advanced skills teachers, taking further qualifications or publishing material on learning to learn.

A full account of Phases 1 and 2 and their findings are presented in the research reports available from the Campaign for Learning's website www.campaignforlearning.org.uk.

Phase 3

Building on the success of the first two phases of the project, a third larger phase was initiated, aiming to work intensively with both primary and secondary schools in specific areas over three years, starting in 2003. Local Education Authorities, Education Action Zones and other networks of schools were invited in September 2002 to express interest in participating in the project and three of these – Cheshire LEA, Cornwall LEA/EAZ and Enfield EAZ – were chosen, using the following selection criteria.

- A clear commitment to the project in terms of resources from both the cluster as a whole and the individual schools.
- A geographical spread of clusters, representing a range of English regions and a mix of urban/rural contexts.
- A spread of research schools, representing all Key Stages, a range of school types (Specialist, Beacon, Church and so on), a range of socio-economic intakes and a range of current educational achievement (based on Ofsted and SATs/GCSE scores).
- Existing work in the area of learning to learn and research expertise. (The aim was to involve some schools that were 'new' to learning to learn approaches alongside schools where the approaches were more established.)

Support and INSET for the project schools is provided by the research team at Newcastle University, the Campaign for Learning and a regionally based co-ordinator from each of the three areas.

Research aims

In order to build on the findings of Phases 1 and 2 the third phase was initiated to research:

- the relative importance of different learning to learn approaches in raising standards;
- how the adoption of learning to learn approaches impacts on teacher motivation and capacity to manage change;
- whether, and if so how, learning to learn approaches support the development of confident and capable lifelong learners.

More generally the project aims to:

1   Explore the impact of learning to learn approaches adopted in Phases 1 and 2 of the project with a larger number of representative schools and assess how learning to learn can be integrated most effectively into schools more widely, including issues such as:

- how best to link learning to learn in school with out-of-school-hours learning and family and community learning;
- how to assess learning to learn;
- how to achieve transfer of learning to learn approaches into other curriculum areas;
- the potential for and impact of online learning to learn and its fit with other online learning.

2   Deepen our understanding of learning to learn and its application among different groups for different purposes in schools, including:

- the interplay between positive learning environments and effective learning to learn teaching;
- the impact of learning to learn approaches in overcoming challenging behaviour;
- the role of learning to learn in helping pupils manage school transition and transfer;
- the potential for learning to learn approaches in overcoming underachievement among boys and specific ethnic minority groups;
- the impact of learning to learn over time on pupil attitudes, achievement and lifelong learning dispositions and practices.

Research framework

The research framework for the third phase of the project is provided by the 5Rs of lifelong learning: Readiness, Resourcefulness, Resilence, Remembering and Reflectiveness.

The 5Rs for lifelong learning are the Campaign's answer to the question 'What makes a good learner?' or 'What knowledge, skills and attitudes/attributes should a learning to learn approach develop?' While taking full responsibility for this model, the Campaign acknowledges with gratitude the work of Guy Claxton, Bill Lucas, Alistair Smith and Toby Greany on which the model is based.

The cartoons on page 19 offer a visual description of the 5Rs while the table on page 20 outlines the knowledge, skills and attributes of an effective learner. Throughout the project the 5Rs model will be evaluated in the light of teachers' experience of using it.

1 Be Ready

Know why you want to learn something and believe you can do it.

By Christmas I want to score penalties every time.

Why can't I play footie like that?

1. Readiness: learners know how to assess their own motivation, to set goals, to achieve a positive learning state, including their preferred learning environment, and to talk about learning.

2 Be Resourceful

Find out how you learn best. Keep trying out new approaches to learning.

I know I learn best with other people. Maybe Emma will help me.

Before we build the robot I need to have a picture in my head of what it will look like.

I haven't got a clue how to build this thing.

2. Resourcefulness: learners know how the mind works and humans learn, to assess their own preferred learning style, to seek out and use information, including through ICT, to communicate effectively in different ways and to use various approaches to learning.

3 Be Resilient

Keep going and try different approaches when you're stuck.

I can't do this homework, but I could always look on the internet, phone a friend or look back at my notes.

I can't do this homework. I must be stupid.

3. Resilience: learners know how to apply learned optimism, to empathize and use emotional intelligence, to proceed when stuck and to ask critical questions.

4 Learn to Remember

Try to apply what you learn, for example by teaching it to someone else. Use different approaches to make the most of your memory.

I'm going to tell you a story about Queen Elizabeth.

I know I'll remember this better if I draw a mind map.

I don't know how I'll remember this.

4. Remembering: learners know how to use various memory techniques, to make connections and to apply learning in different contexts.

5 Always Reflect

Think back after you have learned something and consider how you could do better next time.

That was a laugh. See you tomorrow.

That was a good gig, but I think we need to practise more before next time.

5. Reflectiveness: learners know how to ask questions, observe, see patterns, experiment and evaluate learning.

The 5Rs for an effective learner

Attitudes/Attributes	Skills Demonstrates ability to:	Knowledge Knows how:
Readiness		
Motivation Curiosity Self-belief/self-esteem Self-efficacy (optimism re the learning outcome, confidence and willingness to take risks)	Assess and manage own motivation towards a task Set specific goals which connect to particular learning Achieve a positive learning state Manage own learning process Talk about learning to learn in relation to a new task	To assess own motivation To set goals and connect to the learning To use a learning to learn language To assess own preferred learning environment
Resourcefulness		
Learning from and with others Learning creatively in different ways Flexibility	Make most of preferred learning style and environment Develop and expand learning repertoire and to harness creativity Find and use information Communicate effectively in different ways	The mind works and how humans learn To assess own preferred learning style and environment To use different approaches to learning To seek out and use information, including through ICT To communicate effectively in different ways
Resilience		
Keeping going Learning under stress Managing feelings about learning and teachers, peers and resources	Persist and apply learned optimism and self-belief/self-efficacy approaches Empathize and use emotional intelligence Use different approaches when stuck	To use learned optimism and self-efficacy approaches To empathize and use emotional intelligence approaches To proceed when stuck
Remembering		
Maximizing own memory Applying learning Practising	Use different memory approaches Make connections Apply learning/use what has been learned, including in different contexts	To use different memory approaches To make connections To apply learning, including in different contexts
Reflectiveness		
Looking back Improving learning and performance	Stop and reflect (e.g. ask questions, observe, see patterns) Experiment with learning Evaluate learning	To stop and reflect (e.g. ask questions, observe, see patterns) To experiment with learning To use different ways to evaluate learning

Action research in schools

Schools were encouraged to develop and evaluate learning to learn approaches that they felt were most appropriate to their needs. Each school was required to produce a hypothesis based on one of the 5Rs and grounded in two lists of research aims developed by the Campaign for Learning.

1   The research will aim to understand:

- the relative importance of different learning to learn approaches in raising standards;
- how the adoption of learning to learn approaches impacts on teacher motivation and capacity to manage change;
- whether, and if so how, learning to learn approaches support the development of confident and capable lifelong learners.

2   In addition, the research will aim to understand:

- whether, and if so how, learning to learn approaches can help break down differences in achievement within schools;
- whether, and if so how, learning to learn approaches can help overcome underachievement and challenging behaviour;
- the impact of different leadership approaches in supporting learning to learn;
- the role and impact of ICT in supporting learning to learn and vice versa;
- the nature and impact of different learning environments on achievement and the teaching and learning approaches that best support them;
- the role of assessment in developing learning to learn and how learning to learn can best be assessed;
- the role of the wider school community, out-of-school-hours learning and family and community learning in supporting learning to learn.

Analysis of the school projects showed that there were clusters around the focus on 'the development of confident and capable lifelong learners', 'raising standards' and 'overcoming underachievement and challenging behaviour'. In this first year of Phase 3 of the project, resourcefulness and readiness were the most commonly investigated of the 5Rs. Many schools indicated, however, that they were investigating more than one R and some highlighted all five.

Further analysis indicates that particular project aims from lists one and two are more likely to be linked with specific Rs: schools focusing on the development of lifelong learners or the role of different learning environments tend to mention resourcefulness and reflection, while the goal of raising standards is linked to readiness as well as reflection. The aim of tackling underachievement and challenging behaviour draws on all the Rs, suggesting that the causes are perceived by teachers as more complex and needing multiple approaches.

The key research areas that the project teachers feel are most central to their research to date are:

- how learning to learn can help tackle underachievement;
- how learning to learn can help deal with challenging behaviour;
- how learning to learn can help break down differences within schools;
- the impact of different learning environments on learning.

A number of other areas have been identified for further research in future, including ICT and the role of leadership.

Collecting evidence

In collecting evidence the schools were encouraged to use at least three data collection tools and to include both quantitative and qualitative methods, taking into consideration classroom processes and outcomes as well as the different perspective within the context of the study, such as pupils, teachers and parents. In practice most used more than three methods.

Data collection tools include:

Questionnaires	finding out about pupils' attitudes and what they find helpful/interesting.
Observation	keeping a record (notes/video/audio) of what happens.
Peer observation	a colleague observes and keeps the record for future discussion.
Video	good for later analysis of pupil and teacher behaviours and good record.
Teacher/Pupil logs and diaries	ongoing and regular notes help track the progress of a change and its impact.
Interviews	by the teacher or a colleague – helps explore how pupils feel about the change.
Assessment tasks	tasks designed to assess specific skills, knowledge and understanding – can be used before, during and after the change for comparison.
Pupils' views	recording the impact and changes pupils have detected on their learning since the introduction of learning to learn approaches.
Pupils' work	evaluating the end product of a lesson or unit of work to assess the impact of the change.

School interventions

So what did the schools actually do? They were all asked to decide which of the 5Rs their school needed to develop and then to decide on the learning to learn interventions they would use. Many schools developed individualized programmes but some trends were apparent:

● formative assessment, based on the work of Shirley Clarke, and Paul Black and Dylan Wiliam;

● Jenny Mosley's model of circle time;

● how parental involvement and knowledge about learning to learn helps pupils' learning and attainment;

● incorporation of their learning to learn approach into specified days in which the curriculum was suspended and the focus was solely on learning to learn;

- looking at talk in the classroom – either paired talk (Geoff Hannan) or co-operative learning (Spencer Kagan);

- there were also a number of schools that took a much more generalized approach – perceiving learning to learn to be more about ethos and the use of multiple learning to learn strategies in the classroom, including accelerated learning (Alistair Smith), Mind Maps®, (Tony Buzan), Brain Gym®, (Paul and Gail Dennison) and multiple intelligences (Howard Gardner).

A large group of schools developed individualized programmes based on their own intuition and experience as well as their knowledge of different published approaches. For example,

- Pennoweth Community Primary School, Cornwall, examined the learning environment and the impact of developing pupils' choice in Key Stage 1;

- in Cheshire, the development of generalized learning skills was explored by John Street Primary School;

- pupil reflection was the focus of Cheshire school Leaf Lane Infants and Nursery School

- teachers at St Saviours Infant School, Cheshire made and developed 'stuck mats' to help children be more resourceful in their learning;

- The Roseland School, Cornwall, looked at single-gender teaching groups;

- Hazelbury Infant School in Enfield is investigating a Personal Effectiveness Programme Initiative.

The table on pages 24–29 gives an overview of school case studies, the year group targeted and the methods used. If you would like to find out more about any of the project schools not featured in this publication, their case studies are available to download from the project website at www.campaignforlearning.org.uk.

LEA	School	Project title	5Rs focus	Key Stage	Focus group	L2L focus	Research methods
Cheshire	Fallibroome High School	Learning Together: Implementing Co-operative Learning Techniques in a Secondary School	Resilience Resourcefulness Readiness	Key Stage 3	Year 7	Co-operative learning	On task/off task observations, teacher questionnaire, project questionnaire, focus group interviews
Cheshire	John Street Primary School	Using the Teaching of PE to Develop Readiness Skills to Enable Children to Learn Successful	Readiness	Key Stage 1 Key Stage 2	Year 2 Year 5	Developing learning skills	Teacher and pupil learning logs, pupil views templates, example of pupil work, spelling test scores, pupil interviews
Cheshire	Leaf Lane Infants and Nursery School	Stop! Time to Reflect	Reflectiveness	Foundation Stage Key Stage 1	Nursery to Year 2	Brain Gym®, tai chi, relaxation and visualization, Mind Mapping® and ICT – digital camera	PIPS and baseline assessment in Foundation Stage, teacher logs, pupil learning logs, project questionnaire, pupil interviews with pupil views template, digital images
Cheshire	Over Hall Community Primary School	Using Multiple Intelligences to Create Resourceful Lifelong Learners	Resourcefulness	Key Stage 2	Year 3 Year 6	Multiple intelligences, accelerated learning and thinking skills	Project questionnaire, teacher log, learning logs, work samples
Cheshire	St Saviours Catholic Infant School	Implementing and Developing 'Learning Mats' and 'Stuck Mats' in Key Stage 1	Resilience Remembering Resourcefulness	Key Stage 1	Year 1 Year 2	Learning mats and stuck mats	Work samples, pupil response records, pupil questionnaires, pupil interviews, teacher interviews, SATs data
Cheshire	Sutton High School	Learning to Learn: A Mind-Friendly Approach to Maths and Humanities	Remembering Reflectiveness Readiness	Key Stage 3	Year 7 Year 8 Year 9	Mind Mapping®, peer coaching and Brain Gym®	GOAL assessment, value added tests, attendance data, project questionnaire, pupil questionnaire

LEA	School	Project title	5Rs focus	Key Stage	Focus group	L2L focus	Research methods
Cheshire	Winsford High Street Community Primary School	Creating Resourceful Lifelong Learners	Resourcefulness	Foundation Stage Key Stage 1	Nursery to Year 2	Circle time	Pupil questionnaire, informal observations, pupil interviews with pupil views template, teacher log
Cheshire	Winsford High Street Community Primary School	Resourceful, Lifelong Learning	Resourcefulness	Key Stage 2	Year 3 Year 4 Year 5 Year 6	Co-operative learning, the accelerated learning programme and CHAMPS®	Informal observations, learning logs, project questionnaire
Cheshire	Wolverham Primary School	Developing Resilience in Pupils Throughout the Primary School	Resilience	Key Stage 2	Year 6	Mind-friendly techniques, multiple intelligences, parental involvement, Mind Mapping® and co-operative learning	Pupils' learning logs, project questionnaire, teacher log, SATs
Cheshire	Woodford Lodge High School	A One-Year Study of Delivering Non-Fiction Texts within a Mind-Friendly Structure	Remembering Resourcefulness Readiness	Key Stage 3	Year 7	Mind-friendly environment	SATs/attainment data, teachers' and pupils' learning logs, informal observation, pupil interviews, parent interviews, target-setting, attendance and behaviour data
Cornwall	Alverton Community Primary School	Raising Self-Esteem through Circle Time in Year 5	Resilience Readiness	Key Stage 2	Year 5	Circle time	Project questionnaire, case study of underachieving boys

LEA	School	Project title	5Rs focus	Key Stage	Focus group	L2L focus	Research methods
Cornwall	Alverton Community Primary School	Raising Self-Esteem through Circle Time in Foundation Stage 2	Resilience Readiness	Foundation Stage	Reception	Circle time	Baseline assessments, staff and pupil interviews
Cornwall	Alverton Community Primary School	Raising Self-Esteem through Circle Time in Year 5	Resilience Readiness	Key Stage 2	Year 5	Circle time	Project questionnaire, informal classroom observations
Cornwall	Alverton Community Primary School	Raising Self-Esteem through Circle Time in Year 6	Resilience Readiness	Key Stage 2	Year 6	Circle time	Project questionnaire, informal observations
Cornwall	Alverton Community Primary School	Raising Self-Esteem through Circle Time in a Year 3/4 Class	Resilience Readiness	Key Stage 2	Year 3/4	Circle time	Project questionnaire, pupil interviews, attainment levels
Cornwall	Brannel School	Learning to Learn: A Whole-School Approach	Resourcefulness Readiness Remembering Resilience Reflectiveness	Key Stage 3 Key Stage 4	Year 7 Year 8 Year 9 Year 10	Learning dispositions, and departmental focus on a 5R	Project questionnaire, department data, pupil interviews, staff interviews, SATs data
Cornwall	Camborne School and Technical College	Assessing the Impact of 'Getting Parents More Involved in School' on Student Motivation and Attainment	Resilience Resourcefulness Readiness	Key Stage 4	Year 11	Parental involvement	Coursework marks and GCSE results, staff interviews, parent interviews, pupil interviews

Learning to learn for life – *research and practical examples for the Foundation Stage and Key Stage 1*

LEA	School	Project title	5Rs focus	Key Stage	Focus group	L2L focus	Research methods
Cornwall	Camborne School and Technical College	Assessing the Impact of a Whole-School Learning to Learn Strategy	Resourcefulness Readiness Remembering Resilience Reflectiveness	Key Stage 3 Key Stage 4 Key Stage 5	Whole school	Learning to learn policy	Staff questionnaire, GCSE results
Cornwall	Kehelland Village School	Life-long and Life-wide Learning	Remembering Reflectiveness Readiness	Foundation Stage Key Stage 1 Key Stage 2	Whole school	Classroom reorganization, environmentally based school curriculum, design SKILLS LADDER, personalized log books	Project questionnaire, parental interviews, staff interviews, learning logs
Cornwall	Lanner Primary School	Using Different Teaching Techniques and Organization to Develop Readiness Skills	Readiness	Key Stage 1 Key Stage 2	Year 2 Year 6	Specific learning to learn focus days: 'Challenge Days'	Digital images, informal observations, staff feedback, pupil questionnaire, SATs results
Cornwall	Pennoweth Community Primary School	The Role of the Environment in Developing Lifelong Learners	Resourcefulness Reflectiveness Readiness	Foundation Stage Key Stage 1	Reception Year 1	Learning environment	Digital images, on task/off task observations, pupil questionnaire, teacher interviews, baseline data
Cornwall	St Meriadoc CofE Infant and Nursery School	Does Introducing Parents to Learning to Learn Techniques have a Positive Effect on Pupils' Achievement?	Resilience Readiness	Foundation Stage Key Stage 1	Parents of children in Nursery to Year 3	Parental involvement in learning to learn	Questionnaire to parents, project questionnaire, spelling test results, SATs data, teachers' informal observations

LEA	School	Project title	5Rs focus	Key Stage	Focus group	L2L focus	Research methods
Cornwall	The Roseland Community School	An Investigation of the Effects of Gender Specific Classes for Teaching Secondary English	Resourcefulness	Key Stage 3	Year 9	Gender specific approaches to learning	CAT data and SATs, pupil questionnaires, staff questionnaire, parental questionnaire
Cornwall	Treloweth Community Primary School	An Investigation of the Impact of Formative Assessment Strategies on Behaviour, Self-Esteem and Attainment	Reflectiveness	Foundation Stage Key Stage 1 Key Stage 2	Nursery to Year 6, with focus on Year 4	Formative assessment	Informal observations, teacher questionnaire, pupil questionnaire, case study of Year 4, SATs data, project questionnaire, SMT monitoring
Enfield	Brettenham Primary School	Developing Oracy in Year 2 with a Particular Focus on Turkish-Speaking Pupils	Resourcefulness	Key Stage 1	Year 2	Multiple intelligences, VAK, paired talk	Case studies of individual pupils, lesson observations, pupil interviews
Enfield	Fleecefield Primary School	The Possibilities of Paired Learning in the Primary School	Resourcefulness Reflectiveness Readiness	Key Stage 2	Year 6	Paired learning	Observations of questioning techniques and on task/off task, pupil views templates, pupil interviews, project questionnaire, teacher assessments, SATs
Enfield	Hazelbury Infant School	Introducing the Personal Effectiveness Programme Initiative (PEPI) into an infant school	Resourcefulness Reflectiveness Readiness	Foundation Stage Key Stage 1	Reception	Personal Effectiveness Programme Initiative (PEPI)	Matrix of children's achievements, individual achievement records, digital images, informal observations, pupil interviews
Enfield	Hazelbury Junior School	Developing Reflectiveness and Resourcefulness in Year 4 Pupils	Reflectiveness Resourcefulness	Key Stage 2	Year 4	Brain Gym®, water, classical music, VAK	Focus group interviews, teacher interviews, SATs results, parental questionnaire, project questionnaire

LEA	School	Project title	5Rs focus	Key Stage	Focus group	L2L focus	Research methods
Enfield	Oakthorpe Primary School	The Talk Project	Resourcefulness Reflectiveness	Key Stage 1	Year 2	Talk programme (10 planned 'talk' sessions)	Transcripts of sessions, project questionnaire, pupil confidence questionnaires, SATs, pupil tracking, video
Enfield	Raynham Primary School	Developing Resilience	Resilience	Key Stage 2	Year 6	Brain Gym®, thinking skills and a range of assessment strategies	Pupil questionnaires, pupil interviews, informal observations
Enfield	Wilbury Primary School	Using Formative Assessment Strategies to Improve Children's Writing or 'Nobody's Brain is Ever Full Up!'	Resourcefulness Reflectiveness	Key Stage 1	Year 2	Formative assessment	Teacher assessments, SATs data, work samples, project questionnaire, pupil interviews using pupil views template, learning logs

Findings to date

The action research investigations during the first year by the schools involved in Phase 3 of the project, which will last for three years, overwhelmingly report positive benefits for the pupils, teachers and schools involved.

These findings are based on small-scale case studies that investigated a range of learning to learn approaches and techniques and this makes it difficult to determine the precise nature and cause of these identified benefits. Most schools used a combination of qualitative and quantitative data collection to triangulate their findings and, while these may not be conclusive, they are certainly indicative that investigating the impact of learning to learn approaches in schools is beneficial and has a positive impact on both teachers' and pupils' motivation and that the teachers involved could identify further benefits in terms of pupils' attainment and attitudes to learning.

Where schools did use a more experimental research approach (such as by having a comparison group) both the quantitative and the qualitative data are positive and indicate clear differences in learning to learn classes compared with those not using the approaches. One school that investigated the use of formative assessment found a positive effect equivalent to an average class moving up from 50th to 23rd in a ranked list of 100 similar classes. Learning to learn pupils also showed qualitatively different responses and understanding about their learning when compared with peers who had not been involved in learning to learn activities.

Pupils

Unsurprisingly, the vast majority of case studies focused on benefits for pupils, often specifically in relation to the project aims but also frequently referring to wider affective outcomes of increased enthusiasm, motivation and happiness in school.

> *The children's self-esteem and confidence has soared and this is becoming more and more evident in their work, particularly literacy. They seem to feel safer in their learning and more willing to contribute.*

Teacher, Treloweth Primary School

The role of the individual pupil has been identified as central to learning to learn. Developing knowledge and awareness of the pupil's own learning is the key feature of both broad learning to learn approaches (such as those that develop knowledge of how they learn) and more focused approaches (such as assessment for learning where they take responsibility for identifying criteria to demonstrate their success in meeting learning objectives).

> *We have different kinds of brains. They help us to learn by thinking different things in different ways.*

Pupil, Wilbury Primary School

Pupils were both formally and informally observed by teachers. The formal observations found an increased time 'on task' or a higher quality of pupil talk. Results show that in learning to learn lessons the pupils were more likely to work collaboratively to answer questions and that there was a more equal spread across the genders as to who answered. This impacts positively on the behaviour of the pupils.

It was evident from teacher assistant observation notes that the majority of pupils kept on task, were keener to continue with their work even during break periods and learned to solve their own problems and collaborate more effectively.

Teacher, Lanner Primary School

Teachers

We also found the opportunity to share good practice and problems encountered with others at the meetings invaluable. It gave us a sense that we were not alone in any difficulties we were having and it was also great to share successes and new ideas.

Teacher, Fleecefield Primary School

There is evidence of a positive impact on the teachers involved in terms of their own professional learning, improvement in motivation and in confidence in using learning to learn strategies and approaches, and increased belief and confidence in the success of these strategies to improve attainment and to help pupils see themselves as successful learners.

Over three-quarters of the case studies talked about benefits for teachers and while many of these mentioned improved teaching strategies and classroom interaction, a significant number talked about changed views of teaching and about opportunities to gain new perspectives by working with colleagues within and beyond individual schools in new and challenging ways.

The children in the two learning to learn classes had clearly accepted the idea that everyone, including the teacher, was a 'learner' and could always improve.

Teacher, Wilbury Primary School

Whole school

The project has had a great impact on staff and pupils; everyone has found a common language to discuss teaching, learning and reflecting. As a relatively new staff, our school has now got a shared vision to work towards.

Teacher, Leaf Lane Infants School

Just under half of the reports mentioned benefits at a whole-school level, perhaps reflecting the fact that some teachers are working in smaller groups within their settings rather than across the school. These comments tended to focus on the development of coherent whole-school approaches, improved teamwork and better school–community relationships as a result of learning to learn. Many of the schools that introduced learning to learn in just one or two classes are now planning to roll it out throughout the school.

Parents

> *I have more confidence in my learning ability and therefore I feel this can only help my child's learning ability.*

Parent, St Meriadoc Nursery and Infant School, Cornwall

The schools that involved parents in learning to learn reported that parents found benefits for their own learning and development as well as their children's and that pupils appreciated more understanding at home of what they do in school.

Ofsted

A number of the schools went through an Ofsted inspection during the first year of the project. Here are some of the observations from these various Ofsted reports.

> *The school expects and promotes a genuine desire to learn through its strong ethos and high expectations. Pupils rise to the challenge with enthusiasm.*

> *The whole school emphasis on improving teaching and learning… has had a notable impact which is reflected in the recently improved tests and examination success.*

> *The programme for PSHE is well established, but has only been included as part of the school's 'Learning to Learn' (L2L) programme for two terms. This decision makes good sense as the whole purpose of L2L is to encourage pupils to know and understand themselves as learners. The programme is already having an impact on pupils' self-esteem.*

> *Recent emphasis by teachers on developing pupils' oral skills has resulted in increased confidence in using the spoken language and led to improved standards. Pupils have good opportunities to develop responsibility.*

Attainment

The impact on attainment will not really show up fully until the end of Phase 3, particularly as many of the schools chose to concentrate on the pupils who will be sitting SATs or GCSEs in the last year of the project, but a number of schools are already reporting improvements in attainment and higher than expected results.

Full findings and related information for Phases 1 and 2 and the first year of Phase 3 are available at www.campaignforlearning.org.uk.

Section Three

Practical experience of learning to learn – case studies from the Foundation Stage and Key Stage 1

The DfES materials for the Primary National Strategy highlight the importance of children's experience of the Foundation Stage and Key Stage 1.

In general, though, those that do well early do even better later in life, while those that do not perform well fall further behind; and the chances of breaking out of this cycle of underachievement reduce with age.

DfES, 2004b

It is vital that we engage children in learning early in their education. Many of the Learning to Learn project schools are situated in deprived areas and have identified how learning to learn can help tackle underachievement and help deal with challenging behaviour as their research focuses.

As important is the involvement of parents in their children's education. Professor Charles Desforges with Alberto Abouchaar undertook a review of literature into the impact of parental involvement for the Department for Education and Skills in 2003. This review found that:

● *parental involvement in the early years has a significant impact on their children's cognitive development and literacy and numeracy skills;*

● *parental involvement has a significant impact on pupil achievement throughout their schooling;*

● *between the ages of 7 and 16 the impact is more powerful than social class, the size of the family or the level of parental education;*

● *educational failure is increased by lack of parental interest in their child's schooling;*

● *a father's interest in their child's education has a strong impact on educational outcomes.*

The case study from St Meriadoc on pages 75–86 shows how the school has boosted parental involvement through learning to learn.

It may be useful to look at the case studies bearing in mind that the core principles for teaching and learning in the *Excellence and Enjoyment: A strategy for primary schools* (DfES, 2003) are:

*   *set high expectations and give every learner confidence they can succeed;*
*   *establish what learners already know and build on it;*
*   *structure and pace the learning experience to make it challenging and enjoyable;*
*   *inspire learning through a passion for the subject;*
*   *make individuals active partners in their learning;*
*   *develop learning skills and personal qualities.*

The case studies in this section provide examples of how these principles can be put into practice. We hope that you will be inspired by the enthusiasm of the teachers who have written them to try out and adapt the methods they have used to develop learning to learn in your own school. As the case studies make clear, these methods are evolving and expanding but the results that our project teachers have obtained after just one year of a three-year Action Research Project are impressive.

Introducing the Personal Effectiveness Programme Initiative (PEPI) into an infant school

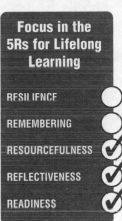

Janet Thomas and Laurel Barber
Hazelbury Infant School, Enfield

The school

Hazelbury Infant School is a large five-form entry school with a nursery that caters for 72 children. We serve a diverse and multi-ethnic community with up to 34 languages being spoken in school. Over 40 per cent of children are eligible for free school meals and a similar number have English as a second language. Just under a third of the children are on the SEN register.

As the Reception intake is 140 plus children, this leaves approximately half without nursery experience. Some of the children attend playgroups but many do not. Others have just entered the country or have just moved into the area. This means that nearly half of the pupils entering the school do not have any prior formal learning experiences.

As many of our children come from backgrounds where English is a second language, some have little understanding of English on entry to Reception. The children may come from homes where parents have difficulty in supporting their education either through lack of English or a limited educational experience or both. Many of our families experience a range of difficulties. Their children may need support with emotional and behavioural issues.

The children are very lively and overall enjoy school and learning. They learn best using a range of teaching strategies. They present a range of challenges to all staff, most importantly to develop the skills needed for them to become confident and independent learners, to be confident in a wide range of settings and experiences and to be able to work harmoniously with others.

Personal Effectiveness Programme Initiative (PEPI) and Hazelbury Infant School

The PEPI model was designed by Gordon Bell, a north of England headteacher. The model is designed to allow for the identification, development and evaluation of five core skills:

- presentation
- research
- communication
- time management
- problem solving.

With these core skills a learner can become confident and capable to deal with varying situations.

Gordon Bell set up the programme for his senior school pupils in response to business and employment groups. The groups were concerned about the skills needed in the workplace, which pupils were lacking.

Despite recognition that pupils come out of school with a range of experiences and levels of examination results, the employers were concerned about the general inability of young employees in using basic skills. These included the lack of good time management, the difficulty that young employees had in working and communicating effectively with others, and the inability to solve problems and find solutions.

The PEPI programme was introduced to Laurel Barber in 1999 through membership of Enfield's Education Business Partnership. The model presented was a senior school model but Gordon Bell had developed the model for primary schools. His concern was that a focus on these skills was needed at a much earlier stage of education and that they would support learning even for young children. We began consultation with Gordon Bell with the view to developing a programme at Hazelbury Infants.

Initially, Gordon Bell worked closely with us. He provided INSET to staff on the background and organization of the programme. Laurel Barber began devising a programme with a Reception class. Gradually all classes are adopting the programme.

Hazelbury Infant School is continuing to develop the programme and support materials. The clown logo was in the original programme introduced by Gordon Bell. The clown puppet we use has been modified from an original Kumquat puppet.

The programme used by Hazelbury Infants allows for the identification, development and evaluation of five core skills in Reception class with an additional skill in Key Stage 1:

1 Organization
2 Time Management
3 Working with Others
4 Communication
5 Research

Key Stage 1 additional skill:

6 Presentation.

Why the selected project?

Project aim

Our project aims to:

- introduce a Personal Effectiveness Programme that develops key skills;
- observe, monitor and research the impact of developing key skills on the children's attitude, understanding and ability to learn and so raise standards of attainment.

Many of our children start school with a low baseline in all Foundation areas. A key factor is a lack of development in speaking and listening skills for a variety of reasons not just affecting children with English as an additional language. This influences their rate of progress and their social development.

'Learning' in its widest sense is not part of the daily routine of home life for many of our children. We feel our children need to develop understanding of how to become independent learners through research (finding information) and organizing oneself for learning. They also need to learn how to use their time productively and be ready to learn (time management).

We decided to introduce the Personal Effectiveness Programme Initiative, which focuses on developing communication and social skills (see box opposite). Personal Effectiveness Programmes are used to develop these types of skills with older children. We believe, however, this needs to be a continuous process from early on as a lack of basic skills causes children to struggle with their learning from a very young age.

The 5Rs

The programme is being used to develop aspects of three of the 5Rs as follows:

Readiness

- **Self belief/esteem** – the PEPI programme is based on individuals setting their own targets and identifying and monitoring their own achievements. This promotes an understanding of one's own abilities, gives children opportunities to express how they perceive their own achievements and enables all of them to be included.
- **Assess and manage own motivation towards tasks** – a long-term aim of the whole project is to give the pupils skills needed to become independent learners. Having the skills to understand and complete a task improves motivation and attitudes towards learning.
- **Set specific goals that connect to particular learning** – the PEPI programme is designed to develop skills in the following areas: communication, working with others, research skills, presentation, time management and organization.
- **Set general goals and connect to learning** – initially the project enables children to verbalize their achievements and discuss their learning process. It then moves on to the children understanding how the skills support learning in all areas of the curriculum and school life.
- **Manage one's own learning process** – a long-term aim of the project is to give pupils the ability to approach tasks using essential skills.

Resourcefulness

- **Learning from and with others** – one of the key skills that the project focuses on is working with others, which links with other strategies we are developing using partner work to support learning.
- **Develop and expand learning repertoire and harness creativity** – we aim to offer the children a range of strategies for learning. Children have the opportunity to relate or develop strategies that suit their learning preference or style.
- **To communicate effectively in different ways** – one of the key skills of the project focuses on a variety of ways to communicate.

Reflectiveness

- **Looking back** – children record, share and reflect on their achievements both in class and across the year groups; there is a higher expectation of this as children progress through school.
- **Improving learning and performance** – consistent reflection between staff and children aims to improve performance.

What happened?

The planning stage

A Reception class of 28 children was chosen to start the programme, to monitor its development and to gather data for research purposes. Planning was completed for both Reception and Key Stage 1 as the wider school was also involved in the project. Along with the PEPI structure a variety of learning to learn strategies were used: Brain Gym®, circle time, the learning environment, visual, auditory and kinesthetic (VAK) learning styles and multiple intelligences.

The PEPI programme is designed specifically for our school and the age of the children (see PEPI box on page 36). Each half term a new key skill (organization, time management, working with others, communication and research) is introduced and developed. Developing these skills has to become part of each teacher's practice.

The following planning tables show how the different aspects of the PEPI programme were included and how they fitted into the curriculum.

PEPI planning: Foundation Stage

Term	PEPI skill	Development of skill	Area of curriculum/topic
Autumn 1	None	• Info on PEPI included on curriculum board in both corridors – picture of PEPI and planning sheet • In class – poster of PEPI and label of that term's skill • Info on PEPI sent out on Foundation newsletter – list skills	
Autumn 2	Organizing myself	• Introductory assembly • Posters • End of half term – one-to-one with each child to discuss achievements and fill in appropriate balloon	General classroom or school routines
Spring 1	Time management	• Introduction: PowerPoint presentation in own class • Letter to parents with slip at bottom to record an achievement at home • End of half term – one-to-one with each child to discuss achievements and fill in appropriate balloon	Relates to: • Getting ready for school on time • Getting ready for PE • Lining up • Tidying up at home and school efficiently
Spring 2	Working with others	• Introduction: PowerPoint presentation in own class • Circle time – activities that promote co-operative working • Introducing paired work (peer support) • Paired reading • Playing with others at playtimes – teaching playground games • Activities to do at home with an adult/older sibling • End of half term – one-to-one with each child to discuss achievements and fill in appropriate balloon	• General • Opportunity to work together on multi-cultural projects
Summer 1	Communication skills	• Introduction: PowerPoint presentation in own class • Develop ability to communicate own thoughts, feelings, views and to question to move learning forward • Highlight the range of ways to communicate: verbal, written, body language, drama, art, IT • Develop in interactive play, circle time, drama, dance, story times, IT • Teach children how to represent their thinking through communication • End of half term – one-to-one with each child to fill in balloon	• Class assemblies to parents • Own work • Displays
Summer 2	Research	• Introductory assembly • Using PEPI storybook called *PEPI Finds Out* • Research for science challenge: using books, posters, artefacts, internet • End of half term – one-to-one, fill in last balloon • End of year certificates for all children – organized and funded by Enfield's Education Business Partnership	• Science challenge

PEPI planning: Key Stage 1 – Year 1 and Year 2

Term	PEPI skill	Development of skill	Area of curriculum/topic
Autumn 1	Organization skills	• Info on PEPI included on curriculum boards – picture of PEPI + planning sheet • In class – poster of PEPI + label of that term's skill • PEPI board outside Laurel's room – Key Stage 1 board – changed each half term by Laurel • Info on PEPI sent to parents – newsletter • Introductory assembly – Laurel • Star of week assembly to include PEPI achievements • End of half term – one-to-one with each child to discuss achievements and fill in appropriate balloon	• General classroom or school routines • Achievements, in all skills, must reflect the year group and age of the children and need to have progressively higher expectations • Celebrating success through star of week assembly to include PEPI star of week certificate
Autumn 2	Working with others	• Introductory assembly – PowerPoint • Circle time – activities that promote co-operative working • Work partnerships • Playing with others at playtimes – teaching playground games • End of half term – one-to-one with each child to discuss achievements and fill in appropriate balloon	• All areas • Year 1 – working together on the Christmas production • Independent learning with partners • Peer support • Learning from peers
Spring 1	Presenting myself and my work	• Introductory assembly – overhead presentation • Sharing work with class – highlight good presentation skills • Create areas for children to present or display their work • Use of IT for labels for own work • End of half term – one-to-one with each child to discuss achievements and fill in appropriate balloon	• Own work • Displays • Look at or discuss displays around the school and in class
Spring 2	Time management	• Introductory assembly – PowerPoint • Using time well independently • Staying on task • Finishing tasks • Completing tasks efficiently and on time • End of half term – one-to-one with each child to discuss achievements and fill in appropriate balloon	• All areas of the curriculum
Summer 1	Communication skills	• Introductory assembly – PowerPoint • Highlight different ways to communicate – speaking, writing, painting, dance, drama, IT • Circle time – focus on communicating our needs, feelings • Circle time – activities that develop confidence and self-esteem • End of half term – one-to-one with each child to discuss achievements and fill in appropriate balloon	• All areas + circle time, sharing work, drama
Summer 2	Research	• Introductory assembly • Using PEPI storybook called *PEPI Finds Out* • Research for science challenge: using books, posters, artefacts, internet • End of half term – one-to-one, fill in last balloon • End of year PEPI certificate for all children – organized and funded by Enfield's EBP	• Science challenge

Parents

At the start of the year a letter was sent to all parents to inform them about the project and how they could support their children in developing the skills (Letter 1). A new letter was sent at the start of each half term outlining the specific skill for that part of the term and some tasks that could be completed at home (Letter 2). Activity sheets were also sent home for parents to work with their children (Letter 3 and Activity Sheets 1–4).

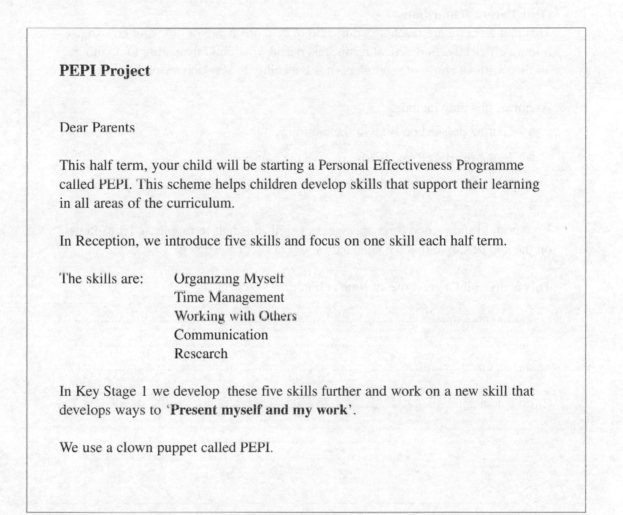

PEPI Project

Dear Parents

This half term, your child will be starting a Personal Effectiveness Programme called PEPI. This scheme helps children develop skills that support their learning in all areas of the curriculum.

In Reception, we introduce five skills and focus on one skill each half term.

The skills are: Organizing Myself
Time Management
Working with Others
Communication
Research

In Key Stage 1 we develop these five skills further and work on a new skill that develops ways to '**Present myself and my work**'.

We use a clown puppet called PEPI.

Letter 1

PEPI Project   **Spring Term 1**

Time Management

Dear Parents/Guardians

This half term we are teaching your child to be more aware of time and how to use it more efficiently. In practical terms, this means your child managing to do things on time without constant reminders. It is the ability to stay on task and finish a task.

At home, this may include:

- Getting dressed on time in the mornings

- Being **prepared** and ready to leave the house

- Completing a job/task at home such as putting their toys away

If your child show good time management skills this half term, please let us know on the slip below so that we can share your child's achievement.

This is my child's good use of time at home:

....

....

....

Child's name: ....

Letter 2

PEPI Project   **Spring Term 1**

Working with Others

Dear Parents/Guardians

This half term we are teaching your child how to learn by working with others. If you would like to work with your child at home, we will be sending some activity sheets that you can do together. We will send a sheet home each week for four weeks. If you return each sheet, we can then share your child's achievements.

Letter 3

WORKING WITH OTHERS – ACTIVITY SHEET

MATHS AT HOME

What is the number of your house? _____

Can you find numbers inside your house? Look for numbers and draw pictures of the things that have the numbers.

Can you write down a telephone number? _____

Can you write down a car number plate? _____

Can you find objects that are these shapes at home? Draw them.

circle   square   triangle   cylinder   cube

Activity sheet 1

WORKING WITH OTHERS – ACTIVITY SHEET

LEARNING THE LETTER SOUNDS

We are learning the letter sound _____ this week. Will you work with your child to find objects/posters/books/pictures that begin with that letter sound. We would like to use them for sharing and for a display in our classroom. Please make sure that nothing sent in is precious or dangerous in class.

So get hunting with your children.

Activity sheet 2

WORKING WITH OTHERS – ACTIVITY SHEET

IN THE PAST – HISTORY

This week we would like the children to learn about the past from you or older members of the family (grandparents).

What toys did your parents/grandparents play with? Draw pictures of them.

What games did your parents/grandparents play when they were children? Ask them to write about them for you.

Activity sheet 3

WORKING WITH OTHERS – ACTIVITY SHEET

IN THE STREET

Can you stand in your street, with a grown up, and draw everything you can see.

Activity sheet 4

Introducing the skills to the children

A clown puppet was used to introduce the PEPI programme to the children. The puppet helped the children get used to the language of PEPI and it brought the initiative to life.

At the start of each topic, a PowerPoint presentation was shown to the children. The presentation showed PEPI the clown learning and demonstrating the skills along with the children. If the children were stuck, they could look at posters on the walls and see what PEPI the clown would do.

Here is an example of how the core skill of communication was introduced to the children.

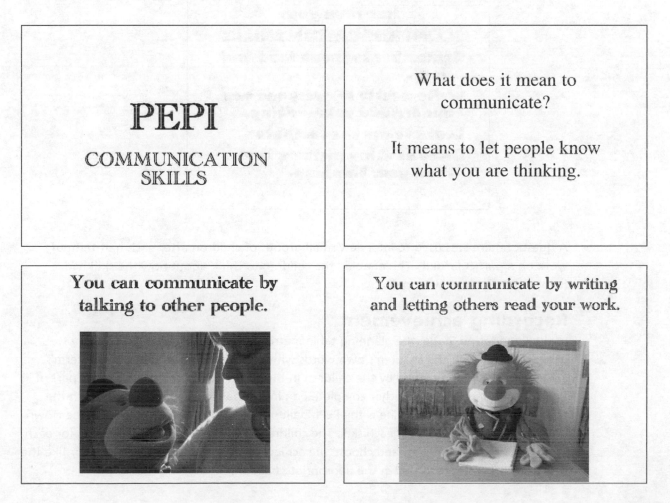

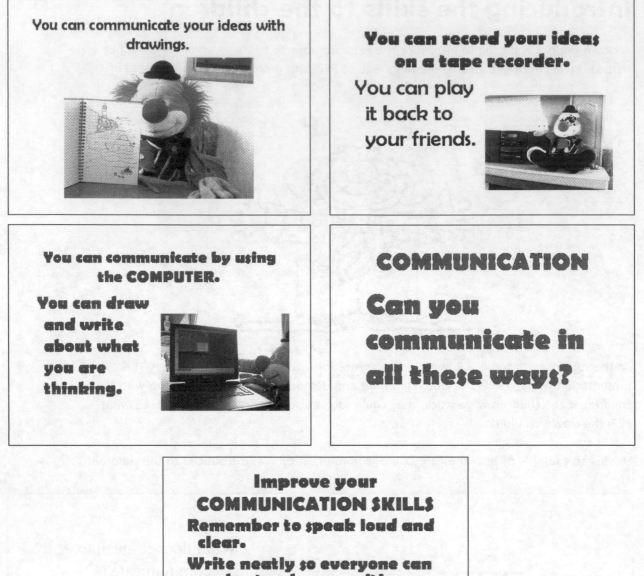

You can communicate your ideas with drawings.

You can record your ideas on a tape recorder.
You can play it back to your friends.

You can communicate by using the COMPUTER.
You can draw and write about what you are thinking.

COMMUNICATION
Can you communicate in all these ways?

Improve your
COMMUNICATION SKILLS
Remember to speak loud and clear.
Write neatly so everyone can understand your writing.
Learn to use the computer.
Draw exciting pictures that show your thinking.

A questionnaire was used to interview small groups of children after each half term of work on a particular skill. This enabled the children to think about how the skill had helped them to complete tasks.

Recording achievement

In the Foundation Stage, the planning table matrix was used to record the children's achievements using the children's own words where possible. In Key Stage 1, the term's achievements were recorded by the children in their own PEPI recording book. As part of the project delivery, each teacher completed an individual achievement record with the children for each skill. Opposite is the PEPI 'balloon' sheet. The sheet shows PEPI the clown holding six balloons, one for each skill. The children look at all their achievements for each skill with a member of staff and choose the achievement they are most proud of or like the best and this one is recorded in the appropriate balloon.

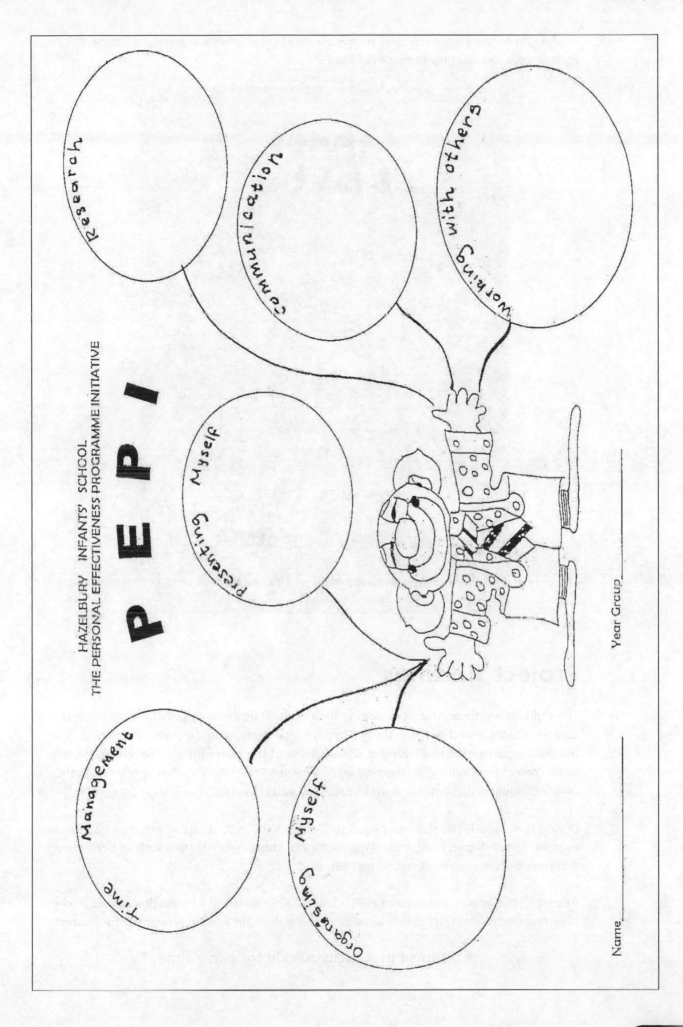

HAZELBURY INFANTS' SCHOOL
THE PERSONAL EFFECTIVENESS PROGRAMME INITIATIVE

P E P I

Research

Communication

Working with others

Myself Presenting

Time Management

Organising Myself

Year Group

Name

At the end of the year, each child received a certificate, sent by the Enfield Business Partnerships, celebrating their work with PEPI.

Project findings

The children are successfully developing their skills. They know their achievements and are able to recognize and describe them. They are also developing an understanding of how the skills support effective learning. Observations of the class indicate that children were using correct terminology to describe achievements. The children's descriptions of their own individual achievements were recorded by adults in class.

During the project, the children began to identify various contexts where they had worked together. They shared their achievements during whole-class contexts such as circle time and class discussions about recording PEPI.

As part of the implementation of PEPI it was possible to see in observations through circle time and discussions that the children were using their time more effectively for example.

❛ I can sit in a circle quickly for circle time. ❜

> ❛ I can get up and go to bed quickly at home. ❜

> ❛ I remembered my snack, water bottle and my book bag. ❜

Children discovered they could do some things more effectively and enjoyably when working with others. This was assessed as part of the observations, in the quotes included on children's individual PEPI records and in discussion as part of circle time.

> ❛ I worked with O---- in dance. We made a dance together. ❜

> ❛ I worked with E----. We made words together. ❜

Some children became more aware of others' needs when working together as these written observations show.

> ❛ One child worked very well with another child using the construction Polydrons to create 3D shapes. One child, an able child in maths, worked with a child on the SEN register. This particular child has one-to-one adult support; however, he showed interest in the activity that another child was doing. The able child was accommodating to the other child and showed him how to make a cube. He then asked the other child if he would like to make a cuboid with him. The children took turns putting Polydrons together and extending their own and each other's learning. One child gained the knowledge of working co-operatively with another child and learning about 3D shapes and the other child learned about working with others and sharing his knowledge. These were great achievements for both children as they were able to use the language to describe their achievement – 'we are working together' – and both children had demonstrated a sense of achievement by communicating with one another, and developing their self-esteem. ❜

As part of the project, children have developed negotiation skills that have been very apparent in the observations. However, they still need focused teaching on communication skills, although these quotes from the children show awareness of communication.

> ❛ I can share my news and talk clearly to the class. ❜

> ❛ I can write neatly. ❜

All the learning to learn strategies used alongside the PEPI structure appear to have had an impact on the children's learning. The role of learning to learn is implicit in the PEPI programme and the process has influenced and developed teachers' understanding of and thinking about the 5Rs and how PEPI supports this.

Conclusion

This is a three-year study so the full impact on the children will only be known when the project is completed. The teacher involved feels positively about the project, however, because its aims are compatible with early years teaching and learning.

After three years we would hope that all teachers will implement the programme well and understand the importance of developing skills that promote effective lifelong learning.

In regard to the children, we would hope that children will continue to develop their skills, will know, recognize and describe their achievements and will understand how these skills support effective learning.

Stop! Time to reflect

Shelley Long and Lindsey Weedall
Leaf Lane Infant and Nursery School, Cheshire

Focus in the 5Rs for Lifelong Learning

RESILIENCE

REMEMBERING

RESOURCEFULNESS

REFLECTIVENESS ✓

READINESS

The school

Leaf Lane Infant and Nursery School is situated on the outskirts of Winsford in Cheshire. The pupils are drawn from a mix of socio-economic backgrounds and nearly all are of white ethnicity. The area suffers from unemployment and is designated as an area of family stress. At 16 per cent eligibility for free school meals, it is broadly in line with the national average.

The Infant School has 196 pupils on roll: 46 per cent boys and 54 per cent girls in seven classes. The Nursery class has 52 pupils on roll: 42 per cent boys and 58 per cent girls, who attend half-day sessions, either morning or afternoon. Pupils' attainment on entry is mixed, but is mainly average or below with particular difficulties noted in speaking and listening, writing and social skills. There are 8 per cent of pupils registered as having special needs and of these 1 per cent have a statement.

Why the selected project?

Project aim

By providing a range of strategies that enable pupils to reflect regularly on their learning we anticipate that there will be an improvement in all pupils' achievement. We asked:

- can children remember and share what they have learned?
- will they begin to set their own objectives for learning?
- does their all-round achievement improve?

At Leaf Lane we feel that pressures of curriculum and the school day have left children and adults with little time to 'stand and stare'. This is an important area of learning on which we would like to place more emphasis. We want our children to have time to reflect on what they have learned, to celebrate their achievements and to consolidate their learning before moving on to the next activity. Teachers were consistently finding it difficult to fit in quality plenary sessions at the end of a lesson and were keen to look at alternative ways to reflect on learning that are appropriate for children in the younger age ranges.

Learning to learn has been recognized by all staff and by parents and governors as a key area to support children in their future learning. Teachers are keen to use a variety of strategies to help children gain confidence and become independent learners. Playing music in the classroom, breaks for Brain Gym® and water bottles have been established throughout the school for some time. Physical activities such as Brain Gym®, tai chi and action phonic schemes are used to support children who need to be active and move around. 'Jolly Phonics' are used throughout the school, for example. Each sound is introduced with a story and an action to help remember the letter sound; for example, 's' is about Sammy Snake and the action is moving your hand like a snake in an 's' shape while saying 'ssssssss'.

The 5Rs

Looking at the 5Rs developed our thinking about the context in which we learn. It opened up discussions between staff, governors and outside experts about what was best for the children at Leaf Lane. Teachers felt stimulated and refreshed by using a range of ideas to improve teaching and learning in the classroom. It gave them opportunities to cater for the needs of children within the national curriculum and it made the curriculum inclusive for all. We decided that Reflectiveness would be an appropriate area on which to focus. By looking back at previous learning we hope to improve future learning and performance. Children will experiment with their own learning and stop to reflect, ask questions, observe and see patterns.

What happened?

A number of INSET sessions were held to introduce staff to new skills, such as working with a digital camera and Mind Mapping®. Teachers with previous experience of learning to learn strategies shared ideas and understanding with all the staff. Teachers in each key stage initially planned together to implement the learning to learn approaches that were most suitable for their age groups.

This was a whole-school approach for Foundation Stage through to Key Stage 1. Teachers introduced the learning to learn strategies gradually with a changing school emphasis each half term. The strategies were put in place across the curriculum and as part of cross-curricular topics.

The aim was to teach the children the key skills they will need to be able to reflect successfully on their learning. An explanation was given to the children about 'reflecting' on their work, 'remembering' and why they were doing the activities in class to support this. Teachers used a range of methods of recording and showing evidence of children's learning in the classroom. The approach was as multisensory as possible, ensuring access for all children and catering for a range of learning styles.

During the year we found different methods to reflect that were appropriate for different age groups:

- Year 2 focused on learner log books and self-evaluation of their literacy and numeracy work;
- Year 1 worked on Mind Mapping® techniques and used these to assess understanding in Foundation subjects that are taught in blocks;

● Foundation Stage used Mind Maps®, with the whole class and recorded learning effectively with the digital camera, focusing more on oral skills.

In the first term, the whole school used Mind Maps® as a tool to reflect on learning. Mind Maps®, developed by Tony Buzan in the late 1960s, provide a way of representing ideas and information visually where links between ideas are represented by branching lines. Drawing a mind maps forces you to find patterns and hierarchies and the colour of the links and the pictures have a visual impact that helps learning to stick. Mind Mapping® enables the learner to see the inter-relationships of facts, ideas and knowledge.

Foundation Stage

When the Reception children used Mind Maps®, they found it difficult to read the words on the branches and so needed more pictures. Instead of individual Mind Maps® the teacher concentrated on making whole-class Mind Maps®.

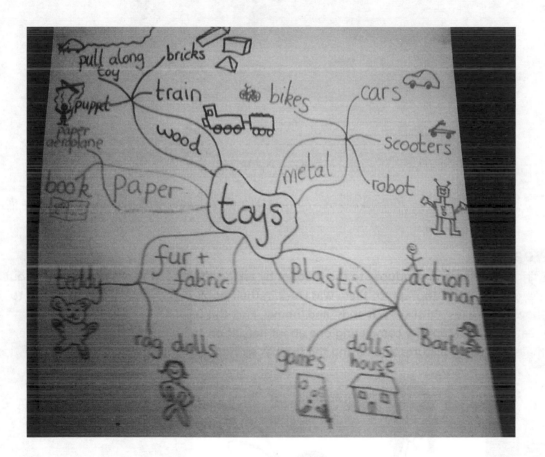

The whole Reception class helped to make this mind map in the Reception class

The children in Nursery started to reflect by first thinking of why they came to school: 'to play', 'to play on the computer', 'so you can dress up', 'to have a snack', 'to work and make things', 'to learn stuff if you don't know anything'. This led onto a discussion about the word 'learn' and it became apparent that the majority of the children did not actually know what 'learn' meant, so further discussions took place to help them think about it. To help the children focus on their learning activities the teacher makes a list on the board using words and pictures or photographs to show them what they will be learning that day and emphasizes the word 'learn' to the children. This also provides opportunities for developing speaking and listening skills. The teacher found that 'Regular reflection with small groups at the end of each session has encouraged descriptions to be more detailed. This encourages children to think more about what they are doing and why.'

Friday
1. Sharing Assembly
2. Make a pattern
3. Magic sand patterns
4. Wooden bricks
5. Castle
6. House
7. Sand

In the Nursery, photographs and pictures are used to identify learning for the day

Year 1

Mind Map... ...m to make a Mind Map® about themselves... ...and they made a mind map to show their... ...acher showed them how to create a M... ...e board and then they made their own... ...writing for them.

Small group work encouraged descriptions to be more detailed encourages children to think more about what they were doing and why.

K...

doughnuts

peas

Mind Maps® became a focus for reflection that could be used at all points in the learning, in particular at the end of the term to see what else could be added to the map and what had been learned and achieved. Large Mind Maps® were displayed on the walls of the school showing, for example, the different ways that the children thought they learned from watching TV, from listening to the teacher, from playing with friends and from using the computer. These Mind Maps® were displayed for the entire year so that the children could reflect back on them. Individual Mind Maps® were included in the children's learner log books.

Children kept their own learner log books to record their own reflection on the process

When asked about using Mind Maps® the children were positive and could see the potential learning value:

> ❛ It helps you with your work when you are looking for things, it gives you advice. ❜

A total of 59 per cent of the children decided that they would rather create a Mind Map® than write. They enjoyed using the different colours and the pictures. The 41 per cent who did not like using Mind Maps® said it was because they did not like colouring in and using mini pictures. This shows the variety of learning styles of the children.

Skills for self-evaluation and reflecting were developed by looking at learning objectives at the end of sessions. The children and teacher discussed feelings about how successful the activity was and what they have learned from it.

A reflection wall

A reflection wall (see above) has been developed to keep a record of what the children feel they have enjoyed learning and what they feel they need to practise more. Photographs are used as visual prompts to help the children.

Year 2

Year 2 focused on learner log books and self-evaluation of literacy and numeracy work. The Year 2 children completed their reflection books at the end of every week, looking back on what they had learned that week. Again, these were introduced by the teacher modelling how to fill them in and then letting the children do their own.

The children used a prompt sheet to help them reflect on their learning at the end of each week (see opposite).

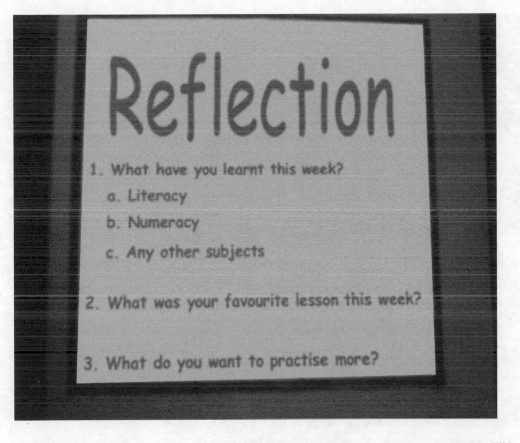

A reflection prompt sheet was used to support the children looking back on their learning throughout the week

These prompts helped children to write up their learner logs. Below is an example of what Rebecca wrote at the end of one week:

1a In Literacy I have learnt about preaficses [prefixes].

1b In numeracy I have learnt about 3 didets [digits].

1c In sions [science] weav [we've] been doing about push and pull.

2   My favort [favourite] lesson was pe because it was rily [really] fun.

3   I want to practes [practice] grids because it was tricky.

The children were able to see the value of this process:

❝ Reflection books have helped us to remember things we have done. ❞

The Year 2 children also reflect on each piece of literacy and numeracy work they do. They have two key questions to think about:

1   Did this work help me to learn?

2   Did I understand this work?

The children use a simple smiley, straight or sad face system to record their evaluations.

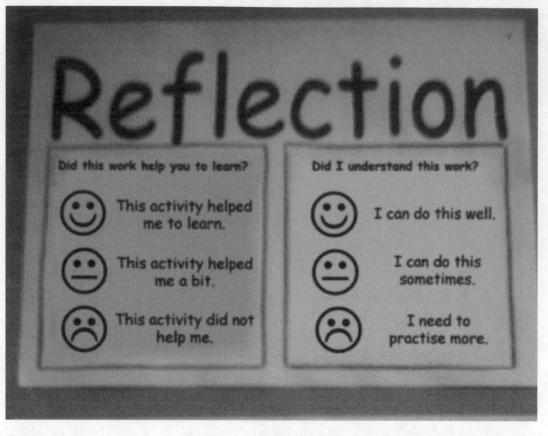

The Year 2 children reflect using this template on each piece of numeracy and literacy work they do

These questions help the children to reflect on their own understanding and also help the teacher to assess and plan for future learning. This can be seen in the comments from children:

❝ The part about what we need to practise tells Miss Heaps things we are not sure about. ❞

❝ It tells Miss Heaps if she gives good enough work. ❞

The teacher commented that:

❝ The red and blue faces also told me a lot about the children's confidence in an individual activity and gave me an idea of the most popular types of activities. ❞

As part of the regular reflection in their learner logs the children comment on what they want to practise more and are therefore involved in setting their own targets:

❝ I want to practes [practise] deaviding [dividing] because I am not used to it. ❞

Teachers

All staff were involved in training for and planning the project as it was a whole-school approach. All staff members were enthusiastic to develop the strategies but there was some concern about the pressures of time and collecting evidence. To help overcome these concerns all staff met together on a regular basis to share classroom practices and new ideas. Information was disseminated by an experienced staff member. The staff were actively encouraged to trial new ideas alongside and through the curriculum subjects rather than teaching them as a separate entity. The research was to be a tool to enhance learning, not something else that had to be added into an already busy day.

The teachers also reflected on their work by completing teachers' log books. These were analysed to see what had been most effective in the classroom and to look at anecdotal notes recording children's and teachers' comments about the learning process. The books were completed approximately every half term or as and when teachers wanted to add something. They were shared at staff meetings throughout the year.

Sharing the learning

Each class, from Nursery to Year 2, takes a turn to share what they have learned with the rest of the school and their parents at sharing assembly. The children were able to use their Mind Maps® to help them to reflect on their learning. They also used digital photographs and the projector to help them remember what they had learned and to help them share this. The digital photographs were particularly useful for the younger children as they provided a record of their practical experiences.

Digital photographs have been important to the whole reflection philosophy of the project

Project findings

The project has been successful in meeting its aims. The children do ask more questions about their learning and are able to look back on and discuss previous learning. The school has established key skills for reflecting throughout the school – Mind Mapping®, language for learning and self-evaluation. The children are able to access a multisensory approach throughout the curriculum and to reflect on their learning.

The children are more aware of why they come to school and that they play an important role in their own learning. They can now discuss what they have learned and are happy to set future goals for themselves. They are justifiably proud of their achievements and have enjoyed having opportunities to reflect on a regular basis:

> ❛ I like reflecting even if I get it wrong. ❜

> ❛ I like listening to other people's work. ❜

> ❛ I feel proud of myself. ❜

Attainment at Leaf Lane School has improved during the last 12 months as recognized by Ofsted in July 2004:

> ❛ The school has concentrated on raising standards and has done this successfully. In the 2003 national assessments, standards in Year 2 in reading and mathematics were average. In the 2004 assessments they were well above average. This improvement in standards is evident not just in the current Year 2 group but also among the pupils in Year 1. ❜

This year's Year 2 SATs results were a great improvement on last year and the Ofsted report commented that Leaf Lane is a 'Dynamic and forward looking school'. The report recognized that:

> ❛ Teachers throughout the school have concentrated on helping pupils learn how to learn. A good range of methods is used to ensure that pupils have opportunities to learn in different ways. ❜

Conclusions

The project has had a great impact on staff and pupils. Everyone has found a common language to discuss teaching, learning and reflecting. As a relatively new staff, our school now has a shared vision to work towards. The project has provided a useful tool for the whole school to focus on teaching and learning. Many informal discussions have taken place in the staffroom, and at the end of the day, sharing successes and failures. The teachers feel positive about the project and the effect it has had on the children, they are able to see how the children feel about learning and assess what they understand. This has enabled them to plan more effectively for individuals.

We aim to develop this approach by extending the techniques used across all ages and to include parents or carers to develop home and school learning. We hope to interview parents or carers at the beginning of the year to look at views of learning outside school and see if active involvement in their children's learning will extend their understanding. From the questionnaires this year it has become apparent that the children see homework as the only learning that takes place outside school. We hope to develop family learning at school.

The role of the environment in developing lifelong learners

Nicola Furnish and Helen Tonkin
Pennoweth Community Primary School, Cornwall

Focus in the 5Rs for Lifelong Learning

RESILIENCE
REMEMBERING
RESOURCEFULNESS
REFLECTIVENESS
READINESS

The school

Pennoweth School is a larger than average community primary school for children aged between 3 and 11 years. The school mainly serves the area of Redruth North, which is deemed to be one of the most deprived areas in the country. It has a roll of 324 with 22 per cent of children on the special needs register and 17 pupils with a Statement of Special Educational Needs (SEN), well above average for primary schools. A small number of pupils speak English as an Additional Language and are at an early stage of language acquisition.

Why the selected project?

Project aim

Our aims for the project are:

- that by enabling children to choose and develop interest in their own learning they will become more resourceful, which will have a positive effect on their own learning and development;

- through reflection time at the end of self-initiated learning children can communicate their learning in a variety of ways – visual, auditory and kinesthetic (VAK);

- that children will develop readiness, through implementing self-initiated learning into the timetable – they will become managers of their own learning;

- that staff involved in the project will feel a greater sense of ownership – they will feel more motivated and will be given greater opportunities for creativity.

Previously the school was structured generally in mixed year groups because of numbers on the roll. The Year 1 pupils were placed across three classes with approximately the same number of Year 2 pupils in each class. As the year progressed it was felt that the Year 1 children were missing out on a hands-on approach to learning. They were taught in a very prescriptive and formal way. As a result, when the children left at the end of the year, although they had made very pleasing progress, there was a feeling within the team that this could be achieved in a more stimulating way.

We decided that in order to offer the Year 1 children a fun and interesting environment to work in, radical changes would need to be made, not only for the well-being of the children but also for the staff, who had felt disillusioned by the existing curriculum and its delivery.

The main objectives were to provide all children with the opportunity to learn through the use of VAK. Other objectives were to provide learning in a fun and stimulating way and to allow children the freedom to develop their own individual interests through self-challenge and self-motivation.

VAK

VAK is an acronym for three learning style preferences – visual, auditory and kinesthetic. Learning styles vary from individual to individual and are a variety of approaches, preferences or methods that learners can take to the process of learning.

The 5Rs

Initial assessments of the Year 1 pupils in September had shown that most of the children were working below the national average. Many were unable to write independently and lacked any real self-sufficiency. A high proportion of the children had not developed a work ethos. This was evident through a lack of pride in their work: many were unhappy doing any real learning and found it difficult to listen or follow even the simplest instructions.

To address these issues we wanted to enable the children to gain greater Resourcefulness and Readiness, to become managers of their own learning and to become excited at the possibilities. We hoped that by offering something unique to each child, they would perceive learning as something that everyone can do and achieve and that they would want to continue to do throughout their lives.

We also wanted to raise staff motivation by enabling staff to be more creative and autonomous in the delivery of the curriculum and to then enrich the curriculum for the children.

With this in mind the following hypothesis was formed: the use of a positive (emotional and physical) learning environment will develop children's Resourcefulness and Readiness, raising pupils' motivation for learning and developing confident, capable lifelong learners while raising standards.

What happened?

The learning zones

A more creative and positive learning environment was devised by setting up three zones that were planned around the curriculum. These allowed the children to visit different learning environments rather than the more traditional approach of one classroom. It was hoped that by giving the children the physical experience of walking to each of the zones various outcomes would occur:

- the first being that the children would be less restless in sessions following the physical move;
- the second being that if the child knew they were entering the literacy zone, by the time they got there they would already be literacy focused;
- finally, having more space to set up resources allowed us the opportunity to place all the resources in each of the rooms so that the children could access their own resources as and when they needed them, thus making them more independent.

When setting up the rooms, time was spent talking to the team about the ethos behind each room. Why are we organizing the zones in the way we are? What do we want the rooms to look like? What changes do we hope to see following the reorganization? Can the children cope and how will they feel? How will it improve their learning? What happens if it all goes wrong? Will the children be more stimulated by the different zones? What learning culture and learning behaviour do we wish to promote?

Room one: the literacy zone

In this zone the whole room is devoted to literacy. There is a large role-play area, resources specifically for literacy and a small theatre. Around the room there are words and posters to stimulate the children's thinking.

Room one: the literacy zone

Room two: the numeracy zone

This room is totally devoted to numeracy. The stimulus around the walls and on the floor is numeracy focused. A role-play area is also in the room to allow the children to problem solve and rehearse the skills they have learned in their learning sessions; even the mat they sit on is numeracy based.

Room two: role-play area in numeracy zone

Room three: the creative zone

This room is organized in two sections: art/design and technology (DT) and science. Within the science area there is a role-play area known to the children as 'the lab' – this allows children to become real scientists and investigate and explore. The other half of the room is devoted to art/DT – all art resources and making resources are displayed for easy access for the children.

Room three: the creative zone – science, art and DT

Learning to learn for life – research and practical examples for the Foundation Stage and Key Stage 1

Self-Initiated learning

Reorganizing the learning zones was a positive move but we were sure that this on its own would not be enough. We intended to make changes to the curriculum. We talked about how we wanted all children to be motivated to learn and how what they were learning would motivate them to want to learn more. In recent years the curriculum has become increasingly prescriptive and generalized to meet the needs of the class as a whole rather than a curriculum designed to meet the needs of the individual learner.

Constraints of the curriculum include, for example, not giving the children the opportunity to explore electricity because they were Year 1 children; under the Qualifications and Curriculum Authority (QCA) schemes they would not cover it until Year 2. We found this hugely frustrating. We felt if one more child was motivated and became excited about learning because we offered them something different, then it was worth making even more changes and so the objective became 'self-initiated learning'.

When planning the self-initiated sessions we had to look carefully to ensure that the children had the required coverage of the curriculum.

Following advice it was felt that we would follow the QCA schemes in the morning and that in the afternoon we would ensure coverage of the curriculum subjects but we would devise our own learning opportunities following Curriculum 2000 as our guide.

		8.55–9.10	9.10–9.55	9.55–10.10	10.15–11.00	11.05–11.20	11.25–12.10	12.10–1.00	1.00–1.05	1.10–1.55	1.55–2.10	2.15–2.45	2.45–3.05	3.05–3.10
Mon	R	PHONICS	Numeracy Room 2	Play Fruit	Science Room 3	MENTAL MATHS	Literacy Room 1	L	R	SELF-INITIATED LEARNING	Play	GUIDED READING 2.15–2.40	ASSEMBLY	Home
Tues	E G	PHONICS	Numeracy Room 2	Play Fruit	PE (games) Room 3	CW	Literacy Room 3	U	E G	SELF-INITIATED LEARNING	Play	CIRCLE TIME	GUIDED READING	Home
Wed	I S	PHONICS	Numeracy Room 2	Play Fruit	Art Room 3	CW	Literacy Room 1	N	I S	SELF-INITIATED LEARNING	Play	LANGUAGE GAMES PHONICS	GUIDED READING	Home
Thurs	T E	PHONICS	History Room 1	Play Fruit	Numeracy Room 2	CW	Literacy/ ICT Room 4	C	T E	SELF-INITIATED LEARNING	Play	PE (games)	GUIDED READING	Home
Fri	R	PHONICS Spelling test	Numeracy Room 2	Play Fruit	Literacy Room 3	CW	ICT (suite)	H	R	RE	Play	PE (games)	GOLDEN TIME	Home

Class timetable

The timetables became far more complex than is traditionally expected. Timing was imperative. It was essential that all staff followed the timetable to the letter, otherwise the children would very quickly become confused, which would result in a loss of learning opportunities. We also felt strongly that we wanted to ensure that no learning session was longer than 45 minutes. There were also a number of other considerations that resulted in the teaching staff and teaching assistants reflecting on the new timetable and adjusting it until we felt it best facilitated the type of learning opportunities we wanted for the children.

In the morning the children were taught in single-year groups of mixed ability but in the afternoon self-initiated sessions they were taught in four groups, each one of mixed ability and mixed year groups: Reception and Year 1. The groups were no larger than 20. Three teachers and two teaching assistants are involved in the self-initiated sessions. Each member of the team supports one of the sessions, with one member of the team having time for planning, resource making and so on. The sessions delivered in the afternoon are history/geography, science, art/DT and music.

	RED	BLUE	YELLOW	GREEN
MONDAY	Science RA – 3	History/ Geography NF – 1	ART/DT HT – 3	Music PS – 2
TUESDAY	History/ Geography NF – 1	ART/DT JA – 3	Music PS – 2	Science RA – 3
WEDNESDAY	ART/DT HT – 3	Music JA – 2	Science RA – 3	History/ Geography NF – 1
THURSDAY	Music PS – 2	Science JA – 3	History/ Geography NF – 1	ART/DT HT – 3

Colour group timetable/Self-initiated learning

Organizing the children so that they knew where they were going was a little more difficult and has developed over the year.

At the beginning of the project each child was placed in a colour group – red, blue, yellow or green – and given a colour badge to wear as a visual aid. These groups were organized in mixed years and mixed ability, so that each group had approximately the same balance of learners.

The structure and planning of the sessions was more challenging and over the year we have gained in confidence and now feel that we have got it right. In each session four open-ended activities are planned. The activities are arranged to allow the children to learn at their own speed. The skill of the teacher in these sessions is not to teach directly but to enable through questioning and to channel and challenge the children's learning and thinking.

Children's choice chart

The four sessions run for three weeks and then four new sessions are planned. Each week the children choose the activity they would like to do and place their name card next to that activity, which is represented pictorially. They choose a new activity every week from the remaining activities they have yet to do. Having four activities planned for each block of three weeks provides the children with a choice at the end of the programme, as there is always one activity left that they are not required to do.

Colour Group Timetable
What are you doing today?

Zone/Area	Room	Colour
History or Geography	1	
Music	2	
Art or D/T	3	
Science	3	

Children's visual timetable

As the year went on, we thought about ways to inform the children as to the zone and session they would be visiting, and introduced a visual timetable for the children to follow. Children now know that on entering their registration room after lunch they look at the visual timetable to discover where they go next. Once they have answered their name in the register, they leave and find their colour group activity. Many people have commented on how independent and capable children of four years old are in following such a timetable without adult support.

Because of the nature of the free curriculum in the afternoon and the more prescribed curriculum in the morning, we thought it essential that the children did not feel a sense of these being separate and disjointed but that they supported one another. This was achieved by establishing each term an overriding theme – for example, pirates in the summer term – and linking all QCA planning and self-initiated planning to that theme.

This is essential and allows the children to make links across the curriculum. We also ensure that the role-play areas support the theme. In the case of pirates, we had 'A treasure chest shop' and 'A pirate ship'.

Role-play area on the theme of pirates

Upon reflection, if we were to start this process again, we may have staggered the changes – first giving staff time to get used to working with the new timetable and learning zones and then after six months introducing the self-initiated learning sessions. Although the children adapted quickly to the changes, the team found dealing with all the changes at once a challenge.

Project findings

What did the teachers think?

> ❝ There are advantages to staff and children alike. There is the ethos that we are all "learning together". Learning to learn encourages children to have a go! ❞

The teaching staff expressed the unanimous opinion that planning for the self-initiated sessions over the week allowed them to be more creative with the curriculum. As a result, staff became more motivated and ambitious in their teaching. They raised their expectation of the children, which allowed the more able children to achieve more, thus raising standards.

> ❝ Yes it is more enjoyable. I like the informal structure. The changing of rooms (learning zones) is innovative for this age group but works extremely well and promotes motivation. ❞

Teaching has become more varied with the use of many different strategies. It is also apparent that the teachers felt they had more time to dedicate to the children and their interests:

> ❝ I now encourage the children to try things rather than just tell them – questioning is very important and enhances their investigations. ❞

Fun as part of the lesson was commonly mentioned and the impact that it had on children's views of learning and school.

Some teachers even talked about how the new approaches helped them feel more confident in teaching subjects across the curriculum:

> ❝ I am more confident and can readily adapt to whatever subject I am given. ❞

The teachers have noted a positive effect on the children through practical approaches used in classrooms, such as movement between classrooms, which gives the children a chance to relax and lets their brains 'breathe', and approaches for keeping them motivated and interested so that they are switched on and focused from the start of the lesson to the fun side of it:

> ❝ as it is hands-on and practical, the children learn through play. ❞

There has also been a positive impact on the children's communication and all children are happy to participate in listening and speaking. The learning to learn techniques have allowed the building of social skills and communication between peers and adults:

❝ Children [are] free to ask questions and help others, taking on a peer-teaching role without arrogance. ❞

This in turn has led to an increase in confidence, self-esteem and independence in the children.

Interestingly, the project was also felt to impact on the children as learners, and more specifically on how they learned. They have a choice in what they learn and at what pace they want to learn it:

❝ The children learn at their own speed without there being a set outcome/ending. ❞

Observation of the class indicated that children had become more motivated in their own learning. Over the year they appeared to become less reliant on the teacher to direct their learning and to keep them focused and on task. The children began to appear excited when making their choice of activity and looked forward to visiting the different learning environments.

	Number of pupils and total time spent on task				
	0–9 mins	10–19 mins	20–29 mins	30–39 mins	40–45 mins
Autumn 2nd	4	2	4	5	0
Spring 1st	2	2	6	4	1
Spring 2nd	0	3	2	6	4
Summer 1st	0	0	4	3	8
Summer 2nd	0	0	0	0	15

Table showing results from on task/off task observations

The same group of children were observed on each separate occasion and it is evident from the findings that there was a 100 per cent increase in the number of pupils who remained on task for the duration of the lesson in the summer second half term compared to the autumn term. The increased age and maturity of the children might, however, have had a positive impact on the on/off task behaviour. It is not clear if this is the case or how much was a result of the positive impact of the learning to learn approaches.

What did the children think?

The pupils were asked 'What do you think of colour groups?' and the results showed them to be 100 per cent positive. Comments such as 'great' and 'cool' dominated. When asked what, if anything, they enjoyed about colour groups, the comments from the students showed that the type of activity was important, with children mentioning the use of Lego® bricks, music, role play, 'moving around the rooms' and 'I like playing with the construction'. One child talked about how the different activities meant they saw other teachers and felt that this was positive. Another indicated that the way activities were presented during this time helped them: 'I like science because it is better than science in the morning.' And importantly one child thought that the approaches are more fun.

When asked whether, given the option, they would like to be in one classroom or have the different rooms to go to, the children were again unanimous in their praise of the latter. They gave many different reasons for this, which included increased interest levels, fun and their learning: 'If I stayed in one room, I would be bored.'

Lastly the children were asked to rate literacy, numeracy, colour groups and science in order from their favourite to their least favourite. Three-quarters of the children selected the colour groups as their first choice.

Conclusion

At present, it is clearly evident that the use of the learning to learn strategy has allowed staff be more creative in their teaching and has, as a result, made them more motivated in their teaching.

It is, however, too soon to make sound judgements regarding whether the learning to learn approach has been responsible for the rise in standards with the Reception children and if it has, by how much. From speaking to the children, however, we can conclude that they enjoy the self-initiated sessions and the different learning zones and that they appear to be more motivated. Further evidence will be collected next year in order to validate these findings.

We intend to develop this project further by improving and extending the planning of the self-initiated sessions to offer more hands-on, stimulating learning opportunities. We will also be looking carefully as to how the children can reflect on their own learning and how the use of ICT could support this in the form of hand-held video cameras to record children learning.

Does introducing parents to learning to learn techniques have a positive effect on pupils' achievement?

Linda Stephens
St Meriadoc Church of England Nursery and Infant School, Cornwall

The school

St Meriadoc Church of England Nursery and Infant School has a two-form entry and a total of 155 pupils plus 38 part-time in the Nursery. The school is situated in an area of high unemployment and poverty and for the past four years has been part of an education action zone. Although as a Church school we take children from a wide area, the majority of our children live near the school. Of the 104 children at Key Stage 1, 20 per cent are on the special needs register and of the 89 Foundation Stage pupils, 30 per cent are of concern to the teacher for various reasons. Eighteen per cent of the children are eligible for free school meals, although this figure would be higher if we took into account the number of our part-time children.

The catchment area of the school is one where academic aspirations and attainment are traditionally very low and the number of 16 year olds who leave school with five GCSE grades A–C is well below the national average. We also have a very high incidence of teenage pregnancies and families with major social problems. Although the vast majority of our parents want the best for their children, many have quite low expectations of their academic ability and potential. Until the last couple of years our Key Stage 1 test results were below the national average.

Why the selected project?

Project aim

To discover whether involving parents and introducing them to various learning to learn approaches will develop their children's self esteem and resilience as learners and so raise standards.

We feel that much of how a child performs in school has to do with confidence, self-esteem and self-belief and that, for the most part, parents have a greater influence in these areas than we do. We realize that people living in this area have low self-esteem and aspirations when it comes to academic achievement and that this is reflected in the way their children perform in school. By improving the self-esteem of the parents we aim to improve the self-esteem and aspirations of the children and thus make them ready to learn. From the outset our aim was to educate the parents and we realized that this was a long-term goal and any benefits gained by the children in terms of improved learning might not be immediately obvious. We would monitor the impact that the parents' involvement had on the confidence and capability of their children and also equally importantly on their own self-esteem and the way in which they perceived themselves as learners.

The 5Rs

In relation to the 5Rs research framework the project aims to improve the Resilience and Readiness of the pupils.

Readiness will be developed through the improved self-esteem, confidence and aspirations of the parents reflecting on to their children. This will help put the children in the right mindset to learn.

Resilience will be developed in the children by educating parents about the importance of self-esteem, self-talk and persevering when stuck and by giving them strategies to help them and their children become better learners. By turning parents into lifelong learners we were hoping to do the same for their children. In the short term we aimed for improved performance in school and greater parental involvement and support.

What happened?

To engage the parents it was decided to hold a series of nine evening sessions to introduce them to the major learning to learn approaches. These were held in the school hall every fortnight starting in October and continuing into the spring term. Although we usually have a reasonable number of parents attending special 'one-off' evenings explaining various areas of the curriculum – for example, literacy or numeracy – other meetings are usually poorly attended and we only have a very small number of parents who regularly come to parent–teacher meetings. We were therefore very uncertain about how many parents would commit themselves to a series of meetings.

It was agreed that the best time to hold the meetings was in the evenings because more people would have a chance of attending and also some of the speakers were not available during the day. This proved to be a good choice as although some people said that they could not attend because of childcare commitments, most parents managed to find babysitters and in some cases both parents were able to come.

The invitation opposite was sent out to all parents of children in our school.

ST MERIADOC C OF E NURSERY AND INFANT SCHOOL

Dear Parents/Guardians

Over the next three years our school will be involved with the Campaign for Learning's Learning to Learn Research Programme. This is a national campaign which aims to teach pupils of all ages how to learn more effectively and is based on recent findings about how the brain operates. Cornwall is one of only three areas in the country to be involved and our school was specifically invited to be a part of it.

I firmly believe that the involvement of parents in their children's education is of vital importance and so propose to lead a series of evening sessions which will introduce parents to the principles of 'brain based learning' which are being increasingly used in schools.

These should be fun sessions during which you will be able to find out not only how to support and encourage your children throughout their school career but also how you can become better learners yourself.

The first session will be on [date] at [time]. If you would like to attend these sessions please fill out the form below and return it to me or give to your class teacher to pass on to me as soon as possible. If you would like more information please come and see me after school any day except Wednesdays.

I look forward to seeing some of you on [date].

With thanks

Linda Stephens
Teaching and Learning Coordinator

Yes I will be attending the Learning to Learn Parents' sessions on [date].

My name is ....

Please return this form to Linda Stephens in Class 1 before the end of term.

We received a very positive response, in fact almost a quarter of our parents replied to say that they would attend the initial meeting and there were quite a number who expressed an interest but were unable to make the dates chosen. Most of these initial parents attended all the subsequent meetings with between 30 and 40 parents attending each session, representing 50 children.

We set out to be as welcoming and friendly as possible as many parents still have a hesitant or even negative attitude towards school and teachers. We also aimed to keep each session light-hearted and fun, but at the same time informative so that everyone went away feeling that they had learned something. At each session we offered tea, coffee and biscuits and there was time for a chat before we started. The sessions lasted for an hour although sometimes overran.

The first session was led by the school's Teaching and Learning Co-ordinator and provided an overview of learning to learn. Parents received handouts (examples below) detailing the personal attributes needed for good learning, that is, self-belief, resilience and perseverance, the ability to reflect on one's own learning, various techniques to improve memory and so on. We also briefly looked at all the areas to be covered by the various speakers at a later date. In effect this provided an overview of the whole programme and gave parents the big picture about learning to learn.

Brain Based Learning

★ Effective learning takes place when we are calm and alert. Our children will develop into more effective learners when they are presented with high challenge but low threat.

★ The brain thrives on feedback. We need to talk to our children about their work.

★ Revision and review are essential in order to retain information. We need to encourage our children to regularly review the work they have done in school.

Brain Based Learning

★ We need to encourage our children to learn the same information in different ways to make it memorable.

★ Learning takes place at the conscious and unconscious levels. We can help our children to learn by displaying information in their rooms.

★ Expectations shape outcomes. Our children will perform at the level they believe they can. We need to help them to set positive learning goals. We need to encourage them!

Brain Based Learning

How do we learn?

Observing Others

Listening to Information

Looking at pictures

Trial and Error

Role Play

Reading

In order to learn we have to receive information in some form or other. We receive information using our senses.

Sight	——	Visual information
Sound	——	Auditory information
Touch		
Taste	——	Bodily-Kinaesthetic
Smell	——	Information

Anyone can learn anything if given the right techniques, enough time and if they believe that they can.

The 5Rs for learning

1 Be Ready
Know why you want to learn something and believe that you can.

2 Be Resourceful
Find out how you learn best. Keep trying out new approaches to learning.

3 Be Resilient
Keep going and try different approaches when you get stuck.

4 Learn to Remember
Try to apply what you learn e.g. by teaching it to someone else. Use different approaches to make the most of your memory e.g. mind maps.

5 Always Reflect
Think back after you have learned something and consider how you could do it better next time.

What good learners do

- Listen to others
- Work with others
- Think about how well they have done and what could be improved.

If they are stuck they:

- Don't give up
- Think about the question again
- Split the problem into smaller parts
- Remember something they already know that might help them
- Ask someone else
- Do something else and come back to the problem later.

For subsequent sessions we enlisted the help of LEA advisers, advanced skills teachers and independent consultants, all of whom were known to be experts in their field and were good speakers. The topics covered were:

1   Seeing yourself as a learner, which included self-talk and Neuro-Linguistic Programming (NLP).

2   Three main ways to learn, VAK, and Brain Gym®.

3   Overcoming barriers to learning by raising self-esteem.

4   Memory skills and techniques to aid memory.

5   Visual learning including mind maps.

6   The different ways of being intelligent, a brief overview of all of the intelligences.

7   Thinking skills, various ways of promoting thinking, for example by odd-one-out puzzles, mysteries, fortune lines.

8   The importance of talk, in particular using a philosophy with children approach.

9   Formative assessment and reflecting on your own learning.

Although it would have been possible for members of our staff to lead some of these sessions, we felt that involving speakers who were renowned for their expertise in certain areas would have more of an impact. This proved to be the case and many parents expressed their gratitude at being given the opportunity to access high-quality teaching and commented that the sessions were very worthwhile and informative.

Tips to make your evenings a success

1   During the planning stage draw up a list of topics that link with what the children are learning in school. (We were introducing Brain Gym® and Mind Mapping® so we knew that we wanted to include these areas.)

2   Draw up a list of speakers who are known to have expertise in these areas and, as far as possible, make sure they are entertaining and easy to listen to as well as being informative.

3   When booking speakers ask them in plenty of time and be prepared to make changes to your timetable to accommodate them. (We found that we had to be flexible about dates in order to get the speakers we particularly wanted.)

4   During the sessions themselves be as welcoming as possible, have a cup of tea and biscuits, and staff ready to chat to people as they arrive.

5   Try to make the evenings as fun and as informal as possible in order to put parents at their ease. (We found that once parents had seen us making fools of ourselves in Brain Gym® sessions and so on, they were much happier about joining in themselves.) Having a good laugh together has strengthened the sense of community within our school.

6   Arrange chairs in groups around tables so people have a chance to discuss what they are learning. (However, some speakers will have their own ideas of how they want the furniture laid out.)

7   After the first evening send a personal reminder about the next session to each family who made a commitment to attend. Have handouts available for those who cannot attend certain sessions.

8   Allow time for reflection at the end of the session and encourage parents to jot down what they felt they had gained from the evening before leaving.

After the initial sessions

Although we originally planned to have nine sessions, parents requested more, especially in the area of NLP. The teachers involved were very enthusiastic about all the approaches discussed and, as the sessions progressed, became increasingly aware of a sense of belonging among the parents who attended regularly. Both parents and teachers looked forward to the sessions for the camaraderie as well as the learning opportunities. Everyone came away feeling that they had learned something worthwhile.

What is Neuro-Linguistic Programming (NLP)?

NLP is the study of the structure of subjective experience. The approach has drawn on different strands of psychology and linguistics to build a simple set of practices that can assist learning and performance in all walks of life. Essentially NLP involves being clear about what you want and how you might best achieve your goal.

Parents were encouraged to provide written comments and feedback after each session and also to report on any successes they had had implementing the learning to learn techniques they had learned. At the end of the series of talks parents were issued with a questionnaire to determine how they felt their attendance would benefit their children's learning.

ST MERIADOC C OF E NURSERY AND INFANT SCHOOL

Learning to Learn Parents' Evenings Questionnaire

Please tick one box

1 How would you rate your own ability to learn? ☐ Good ☐ Average ☐ Poor

2 Has your confidence in your own ability changed since attending this course?
☐ Increased ☐ Stayed the same ☐ Decreased

3 Has your confidence in your ability to help your children learn changed since attending this course?
☐ Increased ☐ Stayed the same ☐ Decreased

4 Has your attitude towards this school changed since attending this course? ☐ Yes ☐ No
If you answered yes please state in what ways.

....
....
....

5 Do you believe that your child will benefit from your attendance at this course? ☐ Yes ☐ No
Please give reasons for your answer.

....
....
....

6 What do you believe about intelligence? Please tick the statement you agree with most

☐ We have what we were born with and that can't be changed.

☐ We can increase our intelligence by clever teaching.

☐ We can increase our intelligence by using our brain more.

7 Have your ideas about the above changed since attending this course? ☐ Yes ☐ No
If you answered yes please state in what ways.

....
....
....

8 Do you believe that you can learn anything given the right conditions? ☐ Yes ☐ No
If this course has helped you to confirm your ideas about the above please say how.

....
....
....

9 What do you remember most about the course and where would you like to go from here?

....
....
....

Project findings

From the point of view of getting parents more involved with their children's learning, the evenings can be deemed to have been a great success. Not only did we have a quarter of our pupils represented but of those parents who attended 44 per cent attended all nine sessions and 80 per cent attended half or more.

Views from parents

One of our research aims was to discover whether involving parents in learning to learn approaches would develop their children's self-esteem and resilience as learners. It is easier for parents to do this if they themselves have good self-esteem. Of the parents questioned, 65 per cent rated their own ability as average before starting the course but all said that their confidence in their ability had increased after attending the sessions: 'I have more confidence in my learning ability and therefore I feel this can only help my child's learning ability.'

Even after just the first session one parent reported that her realization that both she and her son were capable of learning anything had had a positive effect on him:

> ❛ I told him that I know that he can do it even if at present he is finding it hard. He is now asking to do his homework and is delighted to realize he can do it right. I feel I am building up his self-esteem. ❜

We were particularly pleased to note this lady's comment about the child being able to 'do it' even if at present he is finding it hard as this is fostering the child's resilience, which was one of our initial aims.

It is obviously outside the scope of this research to determine whether children of parents attending this course will gain long-lasting learning resilience but given that most educators agree that parental attitudes and input have the most effect on a child, then it is fair to assume that introducing learning to learn techniques to parents of children who are just starting out in their school career will have a beneficial effect on their self-belief and performance as learners.

All but one of the parents who filled in the questionnaire believed that their attendance at this course will benefit their child. The one who was unsure had attended only three sessions. Also 92 per cent felt their confidence in their ability to help their child had increased. The remaining 8 per cent already had a high level of self-belief, which had stayed the same.

The comments such as 'There are many different ways to teach, everyone is different', 'Learning can and should be fun', 'Less pressure really helps', 'Everything is possible, be positive' and 'We can do it! Everyone can!' coming from parents in an area of traditionally low self-esteem and expectations represents quite a shift in attitude and it is this 'can do' atmosphere at home that in our opinion will ultimately have the most effect on raising standards in our school. However, this will be difficult to quantify until children have been tracked over a number of years.

Effects on the children

Looking at the year's Key Stage 1 SATs results, 66 per cent of the children whose parents attended learning to learn sessions achieved higher than average grades. It is, of course, impossible to draw any conclusions from this as it could be argued that these children would have performed at this level anyway.

What is striking about our school's performance over the last two years, however, is the correlation between the introduction of learning to learn approaches to Year 2 and to parents and the rise in our Performance Assessment and National Contextual Data (PANDA) grades. Last year was the first year we really concentrated on the learning to learn approaches of building resilient, independent and confident learners and our average grades rose from E to A in both reading and writing and from D to A* in maths. This year we have also introduced parents to these ideas and, although the PANDA report has not been completed yet and results still have to be finalized, it is clear that we have maintained the higher standards achieved last year.

On an individual level we can definitely confirm that involving parents in learning to learn approaches has led to an increase in standards for some children. One particular father attended all the sessions and has been very enthusiastic and appreciative of the approaches he has learned:

> ❛ I have found the new approach to homework has had an amazing effect – it is fun and we both look forward to it. My child has come on in leaps and bounds and has gained in confidence… [his teacher] has also found this. ❜

The father photocopied and highlighted his child's spellings for the term, which shows that the child's progression from getting all spellings wrong to getting them consistently all correct directly correlated to his attendance at the meetings.

The highlighted spellings are those the child got wrong

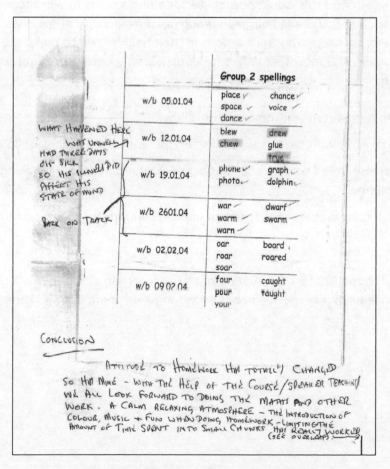

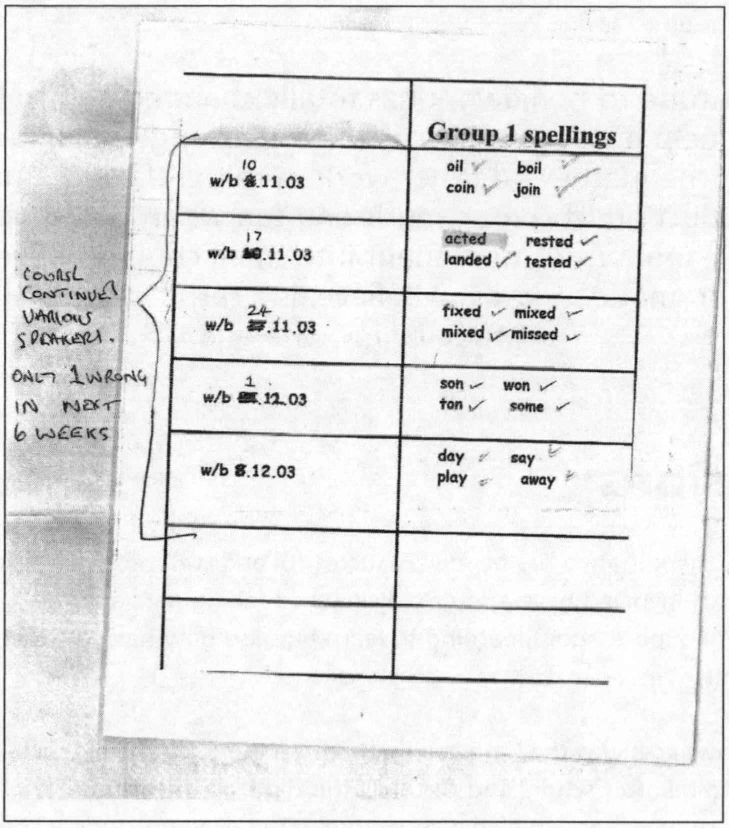

	Group 1 spellings	
w/b 10.11.03	oil ✓ boil ✓	
	coin ✓ join ✓	
w/b 17.11.03	acted rested ✓	
	landed ✓ tested ✓	
w/b 24.11.03	fixed ✓ mixed ✓	
	mixed ✓ missed ✓	
w/b 1.12.03	son ✓ won ✓	
	ton ✓ some ✓	
w/b 8.12.03	day ✓ say ✓	
	play ✓ away ✓	

Handwritten margin note: COURSE CONTINUED VARIOUS SPEAKERS. ONLY 1 WRONG IN NEXT 6 WEEKS

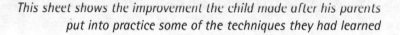

This sheet shows the improvement the child made after his parents put into practice some of the techniques they had learned

	Group 2 spellings	
w/b 05.01.04	place ✓ chance ✓	
	space ✓ voice ✓	
	dance ✓	
w/b 12.01.04	blew drew	
	chew glue	
	true	
w/b 19.01.04	phone ✓ graph ✓	
	photo ✓ dolphin ✓	
w/b 2601.04	war ✓ dwarf ✓	
	warm ✓ swarm ✓	
	warn ✓	
w/b 02.02.04	oar board	
	roar roared	
	soar	
w/b 09.02.04	four caught	
	pour taught	
	your	

Handwritten margin note: WHAT HAPPENED HERE WAS UNWELL HAD THREE DAYS OFF SICK SO HIS ILLNESS DID AFFECT HIS STATE OF MIND. BACK ON TRACK

CONCLUSION

ATTITUDE TO HOMEWORK HAS TOTALLY CHANGED SO HAS MINE — WITH THE HELP OF THE COURSE/SPEAKER TEACHING WE ALL LOOK FORWARD TO DOING THE MATHS AND OTHER WORK. A CALM RELAXING ATMOSPHERE — THE INTRODUCTION OF COLOUR, MUSIC + FUN WHEN DOING HOMEWORK — LIMITING THE AMOUNT OF TIME SPENT INTO SMALL CHUNKS HAS REALLY WORKED (SEE OVERLEAF)

Third example of child's spellings showing attainment after parents had attended all meetings

The father went on to say:

> ❝ M's attitude to homework has totally changed and so has mine – with the help of this course, speakers, teaching we all look forward to doing the maths and other work. A calm relaxing atmosphere – the introduction of colour, music and fun when doing homework – limiting the amount of time spent into small chunks has really worked and M's dramatic progress, I believe, is a result of a total change of attitude by my wife and I. ❞

Conclusions

To summarize, the initiative has been very successful and well received by our parents. The members of staff involved have also greatly enjoyed taking part and feel that not only have they learned more about learning to learn but also now have a closer relationship with our parents.

One of the drawbacks was the time commitment on the part of the teachers as the best time was felt to be after school and certainly this did stop us from putting on more sessions in the summer term, which was very busy. The evenings took a considerable amount of time to organize and co-ordinate.

A possible way around this would possibly be for a few schools to work together and so share the load. This could also help with problems of availability of speakers. We really felt that top quality speakers who were experts in their field helped to make the evenings more of a success. The recent initiatives to set up learning networks might provide a way of doing this.

For us the most important outcomes are as follows.

1   Stronger links with parents who now feel more involved in their child's learning.

2   An increase in self-esteem and confidence among parents that is being passed on to the children.

3   In some cases we can already see an improvement in the child's performance in school.

We have high hopes that a continuation of this approach in our school will result in children who leave our school well on the road to being confident and capable lifelong learners.

Implementing and developing 'learning mats' and 'stuck mats' in Key Stage 1

Fleur McAlvey and Mary Barrett
St Saviours Catholic Infant School, Cheshire

Focus in the 5Rs for Lifelong Learning

RESILIENCE ✓

REMEMBERING ✓

RESOURCEFULNESS ✓

REFLECTIVENESS ○

READINESS ○

The school

St Saviours Catholic Infant School is located in between a council estate and private housing in working/middle-class suburban Ellesmere Port, Cheshire. The school has 132 children on the roll aged between 4 and 7 years with approximately equal numbers of boys and girls. At the time of this research project there were two pupils waiting to be given a statement, about 9 per cent are identified as having special educational needs for learning difficulties and approximately 10 per cent are eligible for free school meals. There are no pupils with English as an Additional Language and a small number are from minority ethnic groups.

Why the selected project?

Project aim

The aim is to produce lifelong learners with the skills to help themselves when stuck:

- we will try to improve the standard of children's writing and to give them more independence by introducing them to different ways of learning;

- we will focus on the 5Rs (in child-friendly terms) during the year to help the children become independent learners.

This project aimed to help the children become more independent writers by developing the use of learning mats (shown in the picture)

Following a fall in writing standards within the school, a development plan was implemented to improve writing across the whole school. The aim was to make the children more independent writers and thus encourage them to improve their performance. Learning mats were designed by the two project leaders with comments and ideas taken from colleagues in response to the learning to learn project and to meeting the aims of the school development plan.

The target pupils for the 5Rs tabletop cards were from Year 1 and Year 2 control classes. Both target classes were used to inclusive learning, mind-friendly approaches, Brain Gym®, water and visual, auditory and kinesthetic (VAK) teaching techniques.

Brain Gym®

Brain Gym® was devised by Drs Paul and Gail Dennison as a tool to prepare a person physically for learning. The exercises are simple – for example, heads, shoulders, knees and toes – but they help to stimulate and energize the brain, and centre and refocus a person. It has been found that this has a positive effect on academic work. Brain Gym® is very useful at low points during the school day when the children are tired and struggling to focus on their work.

The 5Rs

The project aimed to investigate whether using learning mats in Year 1 and Year 2 will help develop their Resourcefulness, Resilience and Remembering, make connections, raise standards and develop confident and capable lifelong learners.

Resourcefulness was chosen as we believe it is necessary to be resourceful in order to be a lifelong learner. We used the mats initially as a resource for the children and realized that it was also an aid to Remembering and to Resilience. We feel that the mats give the children another strategy to become independent learners and therefore fulfil their potential.

Resilience was chosen because we wanted the children to be confident, to keep going and to use different approaches when stuck. Posters and tabletop cards were used to give the children ideas what to do when they were stuck.

It was hoped that the learning mats would make the children more independent by helping them to remember through the use of key triggers.

Photos on tabletop cards were used as a basis for helping children to know the different strategies they could use to approach their learning

What happened?

We decided to tackle the project in two ways.

Our first aim

We began by introducing the learning mats gradually to the children in the autumn term. The learning mats were differentiated and used initially only during the literacy lessons. We hoped that this would give the children a chance to be more independent when writing and would help them to remember words.

Our second aim

We wanted the children to know the different ways of approaching their learning and to know what to do when stuck! We produced a display on our walls that illustrated the 5Rs in child-friendly language. The children were then asked to illustrate how we could do these things after a class discussion into the 5Rs.

We then decided to show the 5Rs on the learning mats using photos of children involved in each learning to learn strategy. This approach was exciting. We could see the children's reaction to the mats was very positive. They enjoyed using them and frequently asked for them when they were writing in other curriculum areas.

We found the research process made us more aware of the children's needs, especially those who were less confident in writing, and what a valuable tool the mat was. After a short time we realized that the mats would have to keep evolving and be adapted to suit more than just the literacy lesson. We recognized this approach could be used in numeracy and many other curriculum areas. As the year progressed we did introduce them in other curriculum areas and always had them available at the writing table.

The 5Rs 'new words' were found to be very useful but could not be seen by the children when they were working without the mats. To address this problem we now have permanent displays in both classrooms with posters on the wall showing the 5Rs in child-friendly terms. We also use tabletop cards which show pictures of the children acting out the 5Rs.

Pupils particularly enjoy seeing themselves on the 5R cards

This has given the pupils the chance to co-operate and work with each other in their preferred learning style. It has also given them valuable tools as they are able to discuss with us what a good learner is as opposed to being good at learning. This is enhanced by a half-hour session with the class each week to discuss what the 5Rs are and how they relate to our learning.

When we decided to produce these learning mats we did not expect them to be so time-consuming to make and adapt – especially if they are to be personalized. It has proved to be quite an expensive resource as photographs have to be updated, words added and improvements made to individual mats and table cards. Thus it was important to be sure of their content before making them. All the mats are in colour and have been laminated to be more hard wearing. This too is an added expense that we considered necessary in order to make the mats more appealing to the children.

Project findings

Our initial aim was to improve children's writing. We have found that the children enjoy their written work more now that they feel more independent. They are showing more confidence when attempting to spell new words or trying to use more complicated language. This has been reflected in an improvement in SATs results from the previous year. It has been very difficult to demonstrate that the mats are improving standards but certainly there is a more positive atmosphere in the classroom that the teachers can vouch for. The benefit to the teacher is that there is more time to spend with small groups of children without as much interruption from the rest of the class.

Questionnaires given to the children at different times of the year show that they think the learning mats are useful and they have become more independent in their writing. Comments from the children showed that they had valued the learning mats in a number of different ways. Some pupils mentioned how they liked the picture representation and they obviously liked the independence that the mats gave them:

❝ Instead of having to think about question words, they are there. Can get letters the right way around. ❞

❝ When you are writing a story it's got to have a beginning, middle and end. It can remind you! ❞

The children also commonly mentioned the benefit that the mats had specifically for writing:

❝ If you don't know how to spell a word, you look at the mat. ❞

Not all comments were positive though. Some children felt that the mats were a reminder of when they were younger:

❝ [Pointed to alphabet and said] don't like it, it reminds me of pre-school. ❞

Or that they did not provide the evidence and information that the individual needed:

❝ Words aren't useful enough. Want long words and hard words. ❞

We produced a working wall display that the children could look at and use to make them more resilient and independent. We have found that the children do look towards the wall, which serves as a reminder as to how to tackle 'stuckness'. The children particularly enjoy seeing themselves on the 5R cards on the table and have made positive comments about them.

Some of the negative effects that we have found were that some of the children got frustrated if words could not be found on the learning mats or they could not read the words in order to copy them. They were disturbing other children who were trying to work independently.

As we have tackled this process as a continually changing project, we are quite happy with the results we now have but foresee further improvements with the continuing use of these learning to learn methods. Adaptations have improved the learning mats and they are now more 'Early Years friendly' because we adapted the language used in the 5Rs so that all our children understand what they mean.

The use of the learning to learn methods has also had a positive effect on the role of the teacher. It has offered us the opportunity to discover our own learning styles and thus adapt to different ways of interacting with the pupils and encouraged us to use mind-friendly learning techniques. It has given us the chance to develop our own skills and expertise and has enhanced our learning.

Conclusion

In summary, the three most important impacts of this project are that we have a very valuable and personal teaching aid/resource that the children enjoy and find useful. Teachers using the mats and tabletop pictures have found that their children are working more independently because they now have procedures in place to activate when stuck, thus enabling the teacher to spend more quality time with a small group of children without being interrupted. We also believe that the children are in the process of becoming lifelong learners as they understand their own ways of learning and have strategies on hand to help themselves when stuck.

The project has been successful on the whole and there is potential for the project to grow much further. We now have plans to introduce the mats and tabletop photos to all classrooms but as we only work in an infant school, our large-scale plans are quite small. We hope in the future to collaborate with our junior school to introduce the project to them. The mats are completely adaptable and therefore could work with all age groups.

The impact of formative assessment strategies on behaviour, self-esteem and attainment

Focus in the 5Rs for Lifelong Learning

RESILIENCE
REMEMBERING
RESOURCEFULNESS
REFLECTIVENESS ✓
READINESS

Ann Webb
Treloweth Community Primary School, Cornwall

The school

Treloweth Community Primary School is situated between the two former mining towns of Camborne and Redruth in West Cornwall, an area of great need. In the last five years numbers on the roll have increased from 177 to 378. There are 25 per cent of pupils who receive free school meals and 48.4 per cent who are currently on the SEN register with 5.8 per cent statemented. We also have 1.8 per cent of pupils whose first language is not English. At Treloweth we have a very high mobility factor, partly because of the recent closure of a nearby school, but overall our stability indicator in the new performance tables was 75 per cent, which is high compared to the national average. All the pupils in the school are involved in the learning to learn project.

We consider teaching and learning to be at the heart of our school and strive to improve provision for our pupils through actively engaging in educational research and keeping up to date with developments, new ideas and findings. We, as adults, consider ourselves to be learners as well as our pupils and continually try to reflect, compare and improve our practice in the classroom. As a result of this we have, over the past few years, introduced a number of initiatives aimed at improving our teaching and enhancing learning.

Why the selected project?

Project aim

The aim of the project was to investigate the impact of formative assessment on learners. Our hypothesis was that implementing formative assessment strategies with primary pupils will help develop their ability to reflect on performance and so develop confident and capable lifelong learners and raise standards and attainment. Particular areas of focus for the study were:

- the development of pupils' ability to reflect on performance by introducing strategies such as Closing the Gap marking;
- the modification of techniques already embedded in our literacy and numeracy teaching into other subjects;

- the promotion and development of lifelong learning skills;
- the impact that all the above have on levels of attainment, motivation to learn and behaviour.

We have been involved in formative assessment since 1999 through the Cornwall Assessment for Learning Project. Working as part of a network with regular support meetings, schools together experimented with different formative assessment strategies and were able to access high-quality in-service training. Having implemented and consolidated the use of formative assessment strategies in literacy and numeracy, the next logical step was to transfer those strategies into the foundation subjects and reflect on their impact and any modifications needed. This work ran alongside the development of Closing the Gap marking strategies in literacy and these were the two main focuses of our staff development programme for a year. They were also reflected in staff performance management targets.

The 5Rs

Many elements of the 5Rs are already embedded into our classroom practice. This has not happened overnight but has been a gradual process. Throughout several years we have aimed to move forward as a whole team with both teachers and non-teaching staff involved. We have taken small steps and regularly given staff time to reflect on their practice and share their experiences as they introduce new ideas. This culture of moving forward together has, we feel, been a crucial factor in our successes. More recently, with our involvement in the Learning to Learn project, we have been able to:

- draw together our many initiatives;
- reflect on how to provide consistency in our approach to learning and teaching;
- develop our practice to reflect the needs of our learners;
- reflect on how to provide continuity and progression in provision for our learners as they move through the school.

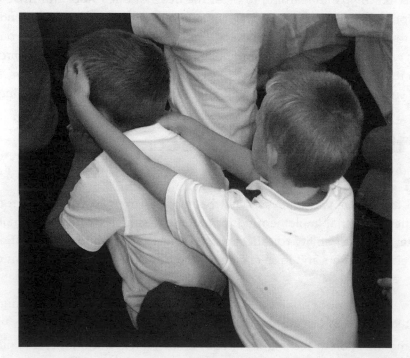

Children using massage techniques in class

Readiness

- We use massage in all classes up to Year 5 and this will extend into Year 6 as the children progress through the school.
- We encourage children to drink water at regular intervals through the day and have provided water bottles.
- We are part of a healthy schools initiative that promotes healthy eating, exercise and so on, we have a healthy tuck shop and are part of a free fruit scheme that extends to all pupils.
- We have a pastoral care system that aims to provide support for children with social and behavioural difficulties and for families. We have a pastoral care team and have employed a pastoral worker.
- We have a team who support pupils with challenging behaviour both within and beyond the classroom.
- We aim to engage fathers in their children's learning through a dads and toddlers' playgroup session and a dads and children's football club.
- We actively encourage the promotion of self-esteem through our assertive discipline policy, circle time and special projects such as Forest Schools, Pyramid Trust and Trailblazers.
- We are currently working with an occupational therapist who is focusing on children who have dyspraxic tendencies and providing a motor skills programme called 'Fun Fit'. Selected children attend sessions before school every day for ten weeks to enhance their fine and gross motor co-ordination.
- We aim to use Brain Gym® to help to engage learners and keep lessons lively, interactive and pacy.

Resourcefulness

- We try to include VAK approaches in all lessons to engage all types of learners and to make children aware of different ways of learning and their own preferred learning styles.
- We encourage the use of response partners to support learners and promote good quality talk in a variety of learning contexts.
- In numeracy we are focusing on developing a more kinesthetic approach using interactive teaching strategies and resources.

Resilience

- We try to foster an atmosphere where pupils see being 'stuck' not as a failure but an opportunity for new learning to take place.
- We provide and discuss a range of resources to support learners when 'stuck' to encourage independence and perseverance.
- We use circle time and our rewards system to actively encourage empathy and emotional intelligence.

Remembering

- We actively teach and discuss strategies for remembering and retaining new learning.
- We encourage peer tutoring to enable learners to consolidate, verbalize and apply their learning to aid memory.
- Our lesson structure is based around Alistair Smith's Accelerated Learning Cycle to promote recall and retention.

Reflection

- We use focused questioning techniques to engage all pupils, stimulate higher level thinking and reasoning and enhance learning.
- Lessons are meticulously planned and appropriately differentiated. They focus on enabling the learner to achieve the learning objective for every lesson.
- We agree the success criteria with the pupils.
- We encourage the use of response or talk partners, thinking time and a 'no hands up' approach.
- We give opportunities for peer and self-marking and opportunities to reflect on progress in both the long and the short term.
- In literacy, we employ a focused marking technique that gives pupils positive responses and a suggestion for improvement based on the success criteria. We aim to provide an improvement time and are considering ways of extending this particular area of work into other areas of the curriculum.

What happened?

Our work in developing formative assessment strategies in literacy and numeracy over the last few years has convinced us of the benefits of these working practices. We implemented the strategies gradually over a number of terms until the following were regular features of lessons:

- Rigorous **planning** to ensure unambiguous learning objectives and success criteria for every lesson with well matched activities and assessment focuses.
- Making explicit to the pupils the **learning objective** for the lesson – discussing how it links with previous and future learning.
- Agreeing with pupils the **success criteria** that they will have to meet in order to demonstrate that they have achieved the learning objective.
- **Effective questioning**, which ensures that learning is developed and extended, and thinking skills employed. This is further enhanced by the use of wait time, no hands up and the use of talk partners to develop answers and engage all learners.
- Opportunities for **pupil self- and peer evaluation** giving pupils control over their learning through the use of a range of techniques including response partners, traffic lights, highlighting or annotation of work, marking ladders (oral and written) and so on. This is extended through the use of pupils as peer tutors, enriching their own understanding by teaching others.
- The use of **feedback** from teacher or peer who acknowledges and analyses successes against the criteria set and provides strategies for improvement.

- The creation of a **positive ethos** and a belief that all students can improve in order to **raise self-esteem** and intrinsic motivation, to enable pupils to see learning as a continuum and to define difficulty as new learning.

- The **adjustment of teaching** to take account of the results of formative and summative assessment.

Using these strategies flexibly to enhance their own practice, staff reported that their teaching was more focused and that lessons were more purposeful. They felt that pupils were more engaged in their own learning and more motivated and that this was having an impact on behaviour. Teachers said they had a clearer view of the developmental stages through which their pupils were progressing and of the ways lessons build into logical sequences of learning. Consequently they felt pupils had a clearer understanding of their own progress not just within lessons, but also in the longer term. They knew where they were going and what steps they would need to take to get there.

Staff discussions now began to focus on the quality of teaching and learning in the foundation subjects since it was generally felt that these lessons were much less effective than those in literacy and numeracy and that both staff and pupils found them less motivating and enjoyable. As a result of the positive responses to our initial work in formative assessment, we decided as a staff that we would like to build on our successes and work on developing ways of applying similar strategies in the foundation subjects. We would work together with colleagues to experiment with the strategies and reflect on any modifications we felt were necessary for them to be effective in different subjects.

At the same time we felt that we would like to further develop our work in literacy by experimenting with Closing the Gap marking strategies, having attended a conference by Dylan Wiliam as a whole-school staff.

Throughout the project there has been much discussion in staff meetings and in-service training sessions about the wider aspects of learning to learn and what this means to both staff and pupils alike. Initially, staff were asked to indicate on a questionnaire what currently happened in their classrooms that might promote one of the 5Rs. This yielded surprising results. The consensus was that we were 'doing it already' and completed questionnaires revealed a very wide range of day-to-day practices and activities, routines and procedures that did indeed promote the 5Rs.

Throughout the year, however, a significant change has been that staff now actively refer to the 5Rs with their classes. Many classes have display boards that explain, at appropriate levels and in a range of different ways, what the 5Rs are and what they mean to us all as learners. Self-help posters and resources are available to classes throughout the school, and pupils have been taught self-help routines to follow when 'stuck'. The vocabulary of learning to learn is ingrained in many classrooms with teachers often referring to the display boards or talking about one of the 'Rs' at appropriate points in their teaching.

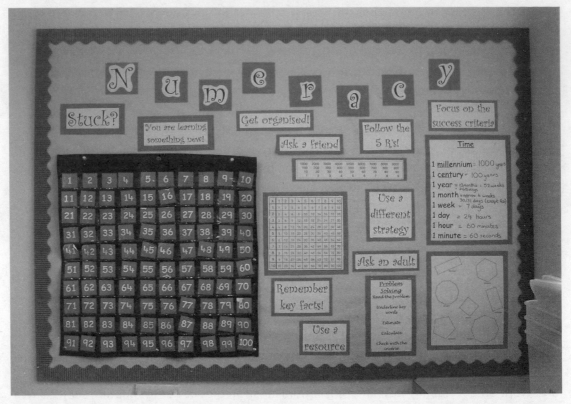

Numeracy display board

Throughout the year our practical investigations into the impact of formative assessment strategies have also given us the opportunity to reflect on our practice more generally. Staff are often asked to allow visiting teachers, headteachers and advisory staff to observe lessons and they do this willingly. They are secure in their grasp of formative assessment strategies and in the wider application of strategies to promote learning to learn. As a result teachers have a clear idea of what the next steps are for their own development and learning, both as individuals and as a whole staff. In this sense the learning to learning culture has impacted on adults as well as pupils. There is also a real ethos of learning among the support staff who involve themselves in the work that the teachers are undertaking at a range of levels, take up a wide range of learning opportunities for themselves and ask for more! Most significantly this promotion of the learning culture has impacted on the pupils – on their motivation, behaviour and aspirations for the future, both long and short term. They are beginning to appreciate the difference between acquiring knowledge and learning new skills, and the impact that the later can have on their ability to learn in the future.

Project findings

A range of activities took place during the academic year 2003–04 in order to provide evidence. These included peer observation sessions, the use of a self-esteem questionnaire for pupils, focused studies and monitoring of SATs data.

The most significant findings of the project were as follows.

- The professional confidence and capabilities of teachers are enhanced by the use of formative assessment strategies – they are empowered by their awareness of their pupils' levels of understanding and their learning needs and motivated by their progress and eagerness to learn.

- Pupils' attainment is enhanced by the use of formative assessment strategies and this is especially true for those of average and below average ability. They behave better, are more motivated and have raised self-esteem.

- The higher-order thinking that the use of formative assessment strategies promotes has a very positive impact on language and cognitive development, which in turn impacts on learning across the curriculum and beyond school.

- The use of formative assessment strategies has a positive impact on pupils' perceptions of their capabilities as learners and their aspirations for the future. It helps to promote a positive learning culture that impacts on the whole school community and school ethos.

Teachers

One Foundation Stage teacher stressed that the development of success criteria with the learners is often more purposeful and meaningful if it follows a period of exploratory or experiential learning. After some time given over to 'trial and error' responses to the task or activity, pupils become aware of steps that need to be taken to achieve success naturally. They then see the purpose of the success criteria and this complex idea is more accessible to them. The same teacher reported that working in this way was particularly valuable for less able children and gave them access to the strategies. She stressed the need for the development of a common language and that in the Reception class they are building the foundation upon which all future learning and 'learning about learning' rests.

Both teachers in Year 1 discussed the importance of developing a 'nurturing climate' to promote emotional intelligence in their pupils, in particular the two key characteristics of successful people that Daniel Goleman (1995) describes in his book *Emotional Intelligence*. One teacher stressed the value of celebrating challenge and encouraging pupils to see difficulty as a necessary part of new learning by the careful use of language and discussion. An interesting observation was that this had had a positive effect on the self-esteem of pupils of different abilities and made them more able to 'traffic light' their work accurately. Where in the past children with high self-esteem would often mark their work with a green light (objective achieved) even though the objective had not been achieved, they became more accurate in their judgements. Similarly, pupils with low self-esteem who would often rate their work with a red light when the criteria had clearly been met became more generous and accurate in their assessments.

The use of think time and talk partners to discuss learning using focused 'prompts' or 'think starters' was felt by one teacher to have had a significant influence on the articulation and evaluation skills within the class. There was an increased level of willing responses, improved quality of articulation and more sophisticated use of language.

Teachers felt that the implementation of formative assessment strategies had also made their teaching more focused and objective led. When planning activities it was seen as essential that these should move the learning on – if they did not then they had no purpose. Lessons were focused on the processes of teaching and learning rather than on the end product. There was greater involvement of children in their own learning at every stage, especially in evaluation of their successes and identification of areas to develop. This was seen to be a challenge in itself and the very involvement of pupils in the process was considered to have an impact on motivation and participation levels.

In Year 2, regular reference to the 5Rs led to a more positive attitude to difficulty, creating an 'atmosphere of willingness'. The use of success criteria motivated pupils to check their work and to make improvements, removing the need to use stickers and other rewards. Similarly the use of marking ladders and response partners were seen to have a very positive impact on pupils' perceptions of their achievements and areas for development. An added bonus was that staff felt that their use of the strategies had impacted on their professional confidence and teaching abilities.

Pupils

All pupils from Year 1 to Year 6 complete a Lawseq self-esteem questionnaire at the beginning and end of each academic year. This shows that for most classes there has been a small increase in self-esteem. It is felt that there were already many strategies in place to promote self-esteem across the school that would have impacted on the first results collected in September 2003. It is possible that the data represents a 'threshold' level of self-esteem and that to enhance self-esteem beyond this level will require a more radical approach, perhaps targeted more towards families, promoting parenting skills and community involvement. It is also possible, however, that formative assessment strategies may have already had an impact on enhancing self-esteem since these were first introduced in 2001 and have been developed and built upon since then.

A comparison between lessons with and without formative assessment produced some interesting results.

Lesson with no formative assessment strategies employed

- The more able children coped very well – they were observed to be using formative assessment strategies without being asked – discussing strategies that helped them, using talk partners effectively – the usual way of working within the classroom seemed to impact on the way they worked from choice.

- Able pupils achieved a certain level with very little teacher intervention – which suggests that they might achieve even more with teacher intervention.

- In the average and less able groups it was interesting that those children who were more successful were the ones who seemed to develop a strategy.

- It seemed to be the less able children who lost out when formative assessment strategies were not used as they were unable to engage with the task with any degree of success. The ability to take risks and develop their own way of working was absent from this group.

Lesson with a range of formative assessment and learning to learn strategies employed

- More able pupils who achieved a lot without significant intervention reached even higher levels of attainment.

- More able pupils consolidated and further extended their learning especially by acting as peer tutors.

- Pupils of average ability adopted the self-help strategies that more able pupils seem to use instinctively and they adopted similar attitudes to learning.

- Less able pupils were able to access more complex learning and their attainment increased.

- Attainment for pupils of all levels of ability was improved but this was most significant for the less able pupils and pupils of average ability.

- There was a significant increase in observed on task behaviours at all levels of ability.
- There was a significant increase in motivation and the adoption of self-help strategies at all levels of ability.

Conclusions

There is no doubt that the adoption of formative assessment strategies and a learning to learn approach in our school has had a significant impact on our pupils, our school ethos, the professional development and confidence of our staff, and the wider school community. This has not happened overnight but has taken a number of years to develop. There have been ups and downs along the way, but our experiences point to two key factors that have contributed to our success and that should be considered when embarking on any school improvement initiative.

Work together – develop a professional learning community where everyone feels valued and able to take risks. Help each other by being a critical friend, observing lessons, planning collaboratively and sharing successes and difficulties. Agree your school improvement targets together so that everyone has ownership. Make sure these are also reflected in performance management targets and work towards them as a whole staff. Involve support staff and the wider school community to raise awareness and understanding about what you are trying to achieve.

Take small steps – do not try and tackle too much at once. Agree to make one small change, try it out, come back together and reflect before moving on. If other issues arise, stop and resolve them while consolidating what you already have in place before moving on.

Using formative assessment strategies to improve children's writing or 'Nobody's brain is ever full up!'

Focus in the 5Rs for Lifelong Learning

RESILIENCE

REMEMBERING

RESOURCEFULNESS ✓

REFLECTIVENESS ✓

READINESS

Ann Mulcahy and Elaine Saini
Wilbury Primary School, London Borough of Enfield

The school

Wilbury is a large, four-form entry, primary school situated in an area of high social and economic deprivation in North London. Associated with this deprivation is an extremely high level of pupil mobility. Compared to national results, the school has relatively low levels of attainment, but the Key Stage 2 results are in line with or above the majority of similar schools.

Two classes of 6 and 7 year olds, 60 children in all, were involved in the project. Overall, the two classes reflected the diversity and range of needs of the school as a whole: from specific learning difficulties to speech and languages difficulties; from behavioural, emotional or social difficulties to autistic spectrum disorder; 43 per cent of children were on the special needs register for a variety of reasons; and they came from 14 different ethnic backgrounds, with 65 per cent having English as an Additional Language.

Why the selected project?

Project aim

Our project aim was twofold:

- to develop reflective learners who would, through the application of formative assessment strategies, learn to assess and to improve their own writing;
- to develop resourceful learners who, through peer assessment, can communicate with others to advance their learning.

In the target group one-third of the 60 children had entered the school within the past year and many of these had had no previous schooling whatsoever. In October 2003, there were 40 per cent with reading ages below their chronological ages, with similarly low levels of attainment in writing. Unsurprisingly, helping children to write was a key priority!

A major initiative in the school during 2003 was the adoption of some techniques advocated by Shirley Clarke for formative assessment. For the Learning to Learn project we took this initiative further to involve the children in the assessment of their peers' written work and their own writing. Sixty children from two Year 2 classes were chosen for intervention, with another two Year 2 classes to act as a comparison.

In addition to improving the children's actual writing skills, we hoped to boost their ability to transfer learned skills to other contexts and to improve their understanding of how they learn – the beginnings of metacognition. These are vital skills, not only for lifelong learning, but also to help raise the children's attainment levels.

The 5Rs

The fundamental objective of the project in its first year was to enable the children to assess their own and their peers' writing. Inherent in this application of formative assessment strategies is the concept of Reflectiveness. A key strategy was developing the children's ability to work collaboratively in assessing each others' work and hence, hopefully, to foster Resourcefulness.

What happened?

Initially the children had to become familiar with a teacher-led assessment process. The teachers presented success criteria in ways the children could understand, that is, 'What will make our writing successful today?' 'What will we get stars for today?' before identifying the pertinent criteria 'capital letters, full stops, finger spaces, extended sentences and so on'. They made the criteria explicit by modelling writing, showing examples in literature, letting the children find them for themselves in texts or by modelling writing with 'mistakes' for the children to spot gleefully, before modelling the 'correct' version: 'I love correcting Mrs X's work... Remember when she wrote the invitation, she never put the full stops or put the comma after the Dear.'

Gradually the teacher gave increasing responsibility to the children by transcribing child-generated text that fulfilled the criteria, using oral rehearsal with 'talk' partners, allowing pairs of children to write together or writing individually.

To achieve all this, given also the low starting levels of the majority of the children, meant a very intensive, highly structured series of lessons. The sequence of lessons on writing a 'recount' for example was as follows:

- A large book *Katy in London* by James Mayhew was read to and with the class.
- This formed the stimulus for the children in groups of three to act out the story of a grandmother and two children let loose in London!
- Initially each group acted out scenarios from the text.
- Then, following a lot of discussion, each group acted out visits to other London landmarks not mentioned in the text.
- The emphasis throughout this was on providing constant opportunities for the children to discuss, share experiences, ideas and vocabulary and be orally secure with this.
- The teacher then chose to be one of the characters and wrote a recount, focusing over three lessons on the introduction, events and conclusion.

- Each section was photocopied so that, working with their talk partner, the children could be helped by the teacher to identify the success criteria for this type of writing; for example, the use of the first person, the use of the past tense, the structure or including personal opinions expressed in the conclusion.

- Over the three lessons, each child wrote their own recounts, working at the end with their talk partner to see if they had achieved the relevant success criteria and for their partner to suggest one aspect they could improve upon. At this stage this was done through the use of a structured assessment sheet.

The same pattern was used in the subsequent lessons where the theme was 'Going to the Fair'. No published text was available for this so there were discussions, oral rehearsals and drama activities heavily based on the children's own experiences.

This time, the teacher's modelled writing (see below) deliberately included mistakes to provoke discussion and reinforce the criteria before the children wrote their own accounts.

A trip to the Zoo   27|4·04

2 First I went on the roundabout with my sister. I rode on a big white horse called Snowy, with tinkly bells on its reins. My sister's horse was called Silver but the saddle was wonky and she was scared she would fall off. We whizzed round and round and up and down at the same time. I felt dizzy but it was great!

1 Yesterday I went to the funfair with my family. I felt very, very excited! We travelled by car but it took such a long time that I thought we were never going to get there. At last we arrived. "Hooray!" we all shouted as we raced to the entrance.

4 Next it was lunchtime. We found a nice shady spot under a tree and spread out our picnic. I was really hungry and ate two chicken sandwiches, a bag of crisps, an apple, three chocolate biscuits and five sweets. "You'll be sick" warned my mum, but I wasn't. Then we all had an icecream. Mine was chocolate and strawberry and my sister had mint choc chip. She dropped hers and my dad had to get her other one.

3 After that my dad took us on the ghost train. It was dark and scary, especially when a ghost reached out and touched my face. That really made me SCREAM! My sister cried.

5 My favourite ride was the Tea Cup Ride. I had three turns on that. It was really exciting when it swung round with a big.....WHOOSH! I had to hold on very tightly so I didn't get thrown out. My dad looked quite scared but my mum enjoyed it as much as me.

7 We were all sad when it was time to go. We trailed miserably back to the car for the long journey home. It didn't seem very far though as we all went to sleep, except my mum who was driving. I had a fantastic day and hope I can go to the funfair again soon.

6. Finally we went into the shop. There were lots of lovely things but they were very expensive. I only had 50p but I bought a very nice pencil with a good rubber on the end. My sister chose a pencil sharpener in the shape of a horse.

Did I choose a good title for my recount? no

Can you think of a better one? The funfair

Did I do my writing in the correct order? no

Did I use any interesting words? Yes Write some of them. exciting strawberry

Did I tell you how I was feeling at different times in my day? Yes

What words did I use for my feelings? fantastic exciting

Did I make you feel as if you would like to go to that funfair? Yes

How did I do this? You made the tea cup ride feel exciting

A trip to the funfair

Yesterday I went to the funfair. With my coson I ast my coson where we are going even when we was in the car. When we came out of the car I spotted the big weel — it was the funfair's. Λ I like this.

First we went on the the gost tran it was very dark and there was sclltns evey where it was scary aspeshly when a gost sat next to me. and said whiooooooo' it made my shot. Then a spide jupped on my head. with a whosh whoshi.

Next we raced to the Teacup ride there was a long queue but it went quit fast froot so we went quid a man came on tolled my that I have to hold on very very tite. It felt me very dizy and sike.

At last it was lunchtime I had som chade cake, a tasty sandwich, andcrisp, My dad had a chikin, Jelly, chikin a berger My sister had some berger, and 5 sweet then

Then we went to the beg weel It was very big When we were on it my baby brother was criing when we got out we went to the a shop I had only 50p I bought a pensul with a god

ruber at the end then went home. I had a greet day.

The example on page 108 is for an average ability seven-year-old boy recounting the trip to the funfair. The boy then had to complete an assessment sheet to analyse his own writing against criteria and how he could improve, below.

Date 28.4.04   Name

How well did I do in my recount?

Did you choose a good title for your recount? Yes

Write another title you could have used. to the funfair

Did you do your writing in the correct order? Yes

Did you have an introduction paragraph? Yes

Did you have a conclusion paragraph? Yes

Did you use capital letters and full stops? Yes

Did you use any interesting words? Yes

Write some of them. scletin skeleton, spotted, raced

Did you write about how you were feeling at different times in the day? Yes

What words did you use for your feelings? sike, dizy

Do you think your friend would want to go to that funfair? Yes

Ask your friend to read your work and tell you what made them want to go to the funfair. She Did like it

Write yourself some advice for next time so you can improve your work.

I could make the end longer

The key features of this process that made it so successful for us were:

- the high levels of oral rehearsal, crucial for all but especially for those with English as an Additional Language;
- the enjoyment generated by skilful teaching, through the drama activities or by letting the children help the teacher to improve her writing;
- the confidence generated by the use of success criteria so the children knew what would make their writing 'good';
- the ethos of mutual trust developed in each class, that they could accept positive criticism from their peers and recognize that everyone was a learner.

These strategies were then progressively continued. The children began to identify the success criteria for their own writing each time, to check their teacher's writing, then their peers' work and then their own against the criteria. Throughout these latter stages the teachers would still be modelling appropriate Closing the Gap strategies, which the children eventually 'internalized' so that they could make appropriate suggestions themselves when assessing and improving their own and their peers' writing.

Closing the Gap strategies are designed to narrow the gap between learners of all abilities. For these Year 2 children, 'closing the gap' became the 'one thing that would make this writing better'. For example, many of the comments initially reflected an emphasis on secretarial skills and presentation: 'Make your writing neater', 'Make your letters smaller' or 'I must leave finger spaces'. Gradually such comments reflected a growing awareness of the importance of the writing's content and of its structure: 'Use more interesting words', 'Don't use and so much', 'It doesn't make sense, I can't understand it', 'You've said the same thing twice' and 'I could have made the ending longer'.

The ultimate stage was to make explicit to the children, as they applied these ideas to improve their writing, the concept of applying one particular strategy in order to 'learn something better': Did they see themselves as 'better learners'? And crucially could they transfer this approach to other subjects and to other areas of their life? In one class they did just this and began to transfer the process to mathematics.

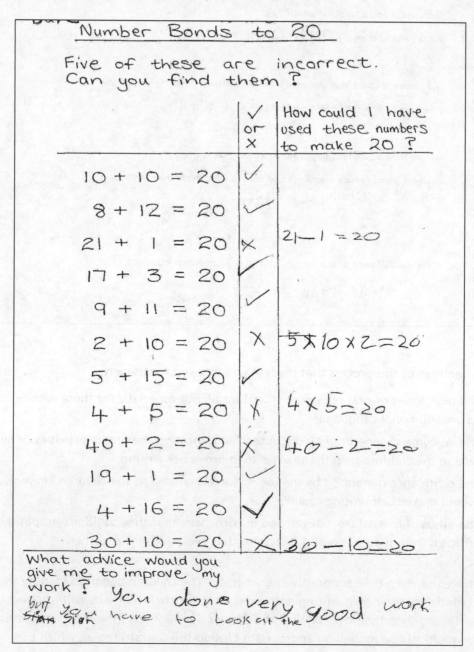

Other evidence of the development of these higher skills was provided by using learning diaries with some children. Initially they were asked to record, three times a week, what they had learned in the literacy lessons. After two weeks, this progressed to the children recording not only what they had learned, but also how they had learned it.

The teacher's analysis of these diaries showed a marked improvement (32 per cent) in the number of more 'reflective' comments by the end of the intervention, with a corresponding decrease in the comments linked to the secretarial or behavioural aspects of learning to write: 'I learned about speech marks so if I want to be a writer when I grow up, I can think back and use them in my book.'

The teacher felt that the diaries showed evidence of the development of reflection. Encouraged to think about how working with a partner improved their learning, children developed from seeing this purely in terms of what they learned to an awareness of how they were learning, reflecting a clear progression of learning skills. This co-operation with and praise from their partner raised their self-esteem and made them happier to learn.

Excerpts from the diaries include comments such as: 'Today I learned to share my Wally book with Christian. He was kind. My partner helped me with a book. He read some of the hard words' and 'My partner helped me by making me feel good. He said he wants me to be his partner again. And that's how he made me happy.'

There was an explicit development of reflectiveness in one class where, through child-friendly vocabulary, the concepts were promoted. The children discussed the ideas and drew their own 'thought showers' to express them

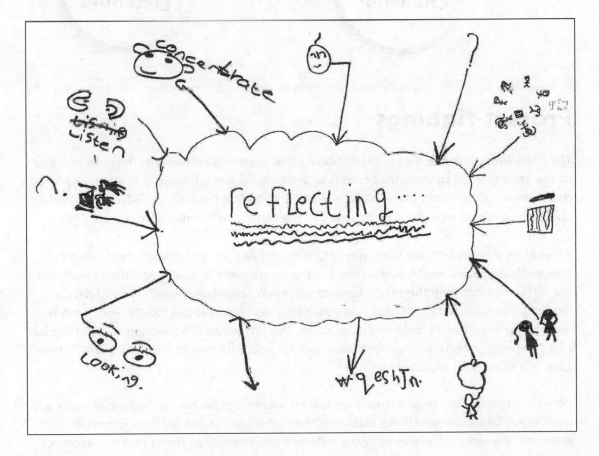

The key words were written on laminated card badges. Every morning the children chose their 'learning word' badge, and at the end of the day undertook a simple oral evaluation of how they had put that idea in practice.

My learning word for today is: **Fun and laughter**

My learning word for today is: **Learning**

My learning word for today is: **Reflect**

My learning word for today is: **Passion**

My learning word for today is: **Care**

My learning word for today is: **Can do / have a go**

My learning word for today is: **Challenge**

My learning word for today is: **Listening**

Project findings

The hard data collected, that is, the national curriculum writing levels at the start and end of the year, seemed to show the benefits of the project. The 60 'project' children improved their writing point scores from an average of 7.9 to 14.9 in the writing SATs. This was well above the average increase in point scores in the other two 'comparison' classes.

An analysis was undertaken using standardized residuals, which for each child looked at the predicted Year 2 level based on the teacher assessments in Year 1 and then calculated the difference between this prediction and what was actually achieved. The difference between standardized gain scores was statistically significant at the 0.0001 level, with the learning to learn classes making greater gains. This difference is equivalent to an effect size of 0.76; in other words an average class using this approach would move up from 50th to 23rd in a ranked list of 100 classes.

Obviously this has not been a strictly controlled scientific experiment. There may well have been other factors at work here, especially the enthusiasm of the teachers involved. However, the more subjective evidence collected also strongly suggests that the approach worked.

There were very positive reactions from the children. Specifically they were able to work with a greater degree of collaboration, to enjoy being in the role of the teacher to help their partner, to easily accept constructive criticism and to feel secure in learning this way: 'When you have partners, you can work better because you have two brains to use.' In contrast, children in one of the comparison classes still perceived collaboration as 'copying', not as a good way to learn.

The children in the two learning to learn classes had clearly accepted the idea that everyone, including the teacher, was a 'learner' and could always improve. Group after group loved correcting the teacher's writing and clearly understood that making errors was an accepted way to learn: 'I just have a go… it doesn't matter if you get it wrong 'cos you are just learning it.'

There was a definite increase in the children's awareness of how they learned. Again the children had begun to articulate this in simple terms: 'Now I think before I write… I use my brain to make it make sense' and 'We have different kinds of brains. They help us to learn by thinking different things in different ways.' This extended to a simple understanding of elements of the 5Rs: 'Today I learned that if you take your time, you will do it.'

They also showed an increased understanding of differing learning styles and the knowledge of how they learn best: 'When I talk it gets my brain thinking. It makes me work better if I talk to my friend' and 'I like reading books on my own to find out things'.

By the end of the year there was some evidence of the transfer of this approach to other areas of the curriculum, even though this had not been planned. The children had little difficulty in their first attempt in offering the teacher advice on how to improve her mathematics work, not just in indicating what was right or wrong, but also in stating the reasons for the errors!

A teacher who was not involved in the project, in evaluating one class's DT, noticed significant improvements in the children's ability to discuss in pairs and a 'let's try it and see' attitude.

What was clear throughout the project was that it needed to be firmly rooted in concrete ideas. Many of the six and seven year olds still found some of the inherent abstract ideas difficult to fully understand. Given the early stages of writing development, many of the children were still seeing how they could improve their writing in very specific terms, that is, 'We must not forget to put in our full stops'. Terms such as 'reflectiveness' and 'resourcefulness' were again too abstract and had to be translated into simpler terms such as 'Have a go', 'I can do it' and so on.

Conclusion

The project for us was very successful. Consequently, we would fundamentally follow the same format and stages: from teacher modelling of formative assessment strategies, to the children applying them to the teacher's work and then to that of their peers, to generating their own success criteria to improve their own writing.

However, we would start certain aspects at an earlier stage, especially adapting the vocabulary of the 5Rs and the use of learning diaries, so that the children were encouraged to think about their learning and had an appropriate language with which to do so. The model is clearly one that would be appropriate to extend, especially into the older age groups.

The most important finding of this project for us was that the adoption of formative assessment techniques by the children themselves appears to lead to higher standards of writing. However, when children are involved in assessing work in this way, they have to be given and acquire other skills – specifically the ability to talk about this process, to use appropriate vocabulary and to begin to separate the 'what' from the 'how' in learning. This, for us, was another significant finding.

Section Four

Developing learning to learn in your school

This section offers some brief general guidance on putting learning to learn into practice in your school. It does not attempt to provide a blueprint or suggest that there is one right way to introduce learning to learn. Every school is different. It is important that whatever you do is appropriate to your situation and takes account of the way you and your colleagues already plan your work but the following cycle may be helpful in structuring your thinking.

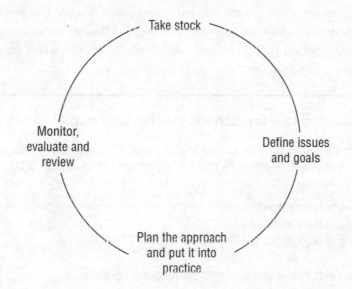

You can find more guidance on introducing learning to learn in *Creating a Learning to Learn School* (Greany and Rodd, 2003).

Taking stock – where are you starting from?

When thinking about how you are going to implement learning to learn in your school, you first need to establish whether this is a school-wide initiative, a project involving just a few teachers or perhaps you are going it alone initially. You will, of course, need management support so that you have time to plan and develop the work. If you are a lone pioneer or one of a small group of like-minded people, do not despair. It may take time for colleagues to get involved but many of our project teachers have found that what started as small initiatives in one or two classes are now being spread school-wide because of their success. Developing projects that are relevant to their schools has had positive impacts on teacher motivation and team working and has made these initiatives all the more effective.

The ethos of moving forward together as a team is currently very strong. It is this feeling of learning together which has helped us to identify our next area of development which will be the use of high quality questioning as formative assessment strategy.

Treloweth Primary School, Cornwall

As well as assessing the level of support and size of the learning to learn team, you might wish to identify other initiatives that are already in place or planned in your school and that will have an impact on or relationship to learning to learn. You will also need to take stock of your school's and your own teaching and learning approach. This may be set out in formal statements such as the School Development Plan or Teaching and Learning Strategy and you will also have a sense of the ethos of the school from your own observations.

Defining issues and goals – where do you want to get to?

Having assessed where you are starting from, the next question is where do you want to get to? What do you want to change and how do you want to change it? Before brainstorming specific issues in your school and agreeing your goals, you might find it helpful to reflect on what makes a learning to learn school and how its teachers and pupils would experience it.

What makes a learning to learn school, teacher and pupil?

We asked a selection of the project teachers to identify what makes a learning to learn school, teacher and pupil. Before looking at what they said think about what your answers would be to the following questions:

- What is a learning to learn school?
- What is a learning to learn teacher?
- What is a learning to learn pupil?

Our project teachers' answers can be grouped under the following headings.

What is a learning to learn school?

- *School culture (such as a focus on teaching and learning)* – focus on teaching and learning, open to change, increase pupil motivation, everyone is a learner, lively or stimulating, high aspirations, good physical environment, parental involvement, raise standards, boost teacher morale.
- *What pupils do (such as being reflective and being prepared to take risks)* – pupil involvement or responsibility, pupils take risks, pupils reflective.
- *What teachers do (such as using a variety of teaching styles and approaches)* – variety of styles and approaches, use research, self-evaluate, common approach/teamwork, positive relationships, broad rich curriculum, clear vision from head, explicit cross-curricular links, creativity.

What is a learning to learn teacher?

- *Effective relationships with pupils* – inclusivity, listen to pupils, role model.
- *Process features (such as talking about learning)* – learning alongside pupils, planning, talk about learning, creative, team player, resourceful.
- *Environmental factors* – positive environment, explicit teaching of learning to learn skills, recognition of learning to learn.

What is a learning to learn pupil?

- *Aware of the process of learning* – process knowledge, self-evaluating, autonomy, resourcefulness, problem solving, remembering.
- *Psychologically prepared for learning* – independence, motivation, reflectiveness, resilience, adapt to change, enjoy learning, self-confidence, empowerment.
- *Effective communicator* – communication skills, work with others, active participation, emotional skills.

How do your answers compare?

Having reflected on the larger picture, the next question is 'where do you want to get to?' The learning to learn team could use the following checklist to help in brainstorming the answer to this key question:

- What are the big issues for learning and teaching in our school?
- What do we want to change and why?
- How do we want to change it?
- Are there particular groups of pupils causing concern?
- Is parental involvement or the lack of it an issue?
- What goals do we want to achieve in the next year and the next three years?
- What will success look and feel like?
- How can we build this into our School Development Plan/Teaching and Learning Strategy/other planning process?

Planning your approach – how will you put it into practice?

Having sorted out the issues you want to focus on and what your goals are, you can now plan your approach and put it into practice. As the section on school interventions on page 22 shows, some of our project schools developed individualized programmes based on their own intuition and experience while others used a range of published approaches. The key factor is your judgement of what will work best in your school. Sufficient time for planning, INSET and review is also crucial.

At this point the 5Rs framework will be helpful. We asked our project teachers to match some learning to learn approaches and techniques to the 5Rs. Many of these are useful for developing several of the Rs.

Readiness	Remembering	Resourcefulness	Resilience	Reflectiveness
Student Aspirations Project	Thinking science curriculum	Circle time	Emotional intelligence approaches	Learning logs
Paired talk	Mind Mapping®	Talk for learning	Assessment for learning/formative assessment	Mind Maps®
Parent education/involvement	MASTER learning cycle	Co-operative learning styles	Mentoring	Digital photographs
Questioning skills	Multisensory learning	E-learning tool kit	Parental education/ involvement	Circle time
Parent education/involvement	Peer teaching	Self-initiated learning science		Use of FA strategies
Using PE		Brainwaves II		Assessment for learning/Formative assessment
Readiness to Learn programme		Using multiple intelligences		
Circle time		Paired learning		
Professional Effectiveness Programme		Learning mats		
CHAMPS				
Activate prior knowledge				

Matching learning to learn approaches to the 5Rs

The 5Rs also can provide a common language that both teachers and pupils can use.

> *The vocabulary of learning to learn is ingrained in many classrooms with teachers often referring to the display boards or talking about one of the Rs at appropriate points in their teaching.*

Treloweth Community Primary School, Cornwall

Monitoring, evaluation and review

As with any new development, you will want to build in ways of checking on progress and using this information to evaluate and review how learning to learn is developing in your school. In addition to hard data from SATs, you may want to consider one or more of the data collection tools used by our project schools that are set out on page 22.

Many of our project schools emphasize the exploratory nature of learning to learn and the importance of keeping teaching and learning strategies under review so that there is continuous improvement.

> *We believe as a school that it is essential to reflect and develop our practice by sharing ideas and keeping informed of new initiatives…aimed at improving our teaching and learning.*

Pennoweth Community Primary School

Of course making all these changes is never going to be easy as some of the schools featured within the book have commented. Pennoweth, for example, would have made the same changes but with hindsight they would have implemented them more gradually rather than all together. Other schools found that combining introducing the techniques along with preparing for an Ofsted inspection was challenging. Changes in key staff impacted on implementation of the learning to learn approach in some schools. Learner logs worked in some of the project schools but not in one.

This all goes to show that each school is different and that it is essential that you develop a programme that is right for you. It is hard work but our project schools are very clear about the benefits.

> *Learning to learn has been recognized by all staff, parents and governors as a key area to support children in their future learning. Teachers are keen to use a variety of strategies to help children gain confidence and become independent learners.*

Leaf Lane Infants School, Cheshire

How to do it in your school – some practical suggestions

As we emphasize throughout this book, every school is different and learning to learn needs to be developed accordingly but you may find these practical suggestions helpful. They come from Ann Webb, Teaching and Learning Co-ordinator at Treloweth Community Primary School, who has worked on improving teaching and enhancing learning for the past few years.

Make the learning objective explicit

- Tell pupils what they will have achieved by the end of the lesson or unit of work. Tell them how they will feel when they get there. Make them aware of how the learning objective links with previous learning – yesterday, last week, last term, last year – and with future learning – 'when you have learned to ... you will be able to ... and this will help you when you are trying to ...'. Give them the big picture and let them know where each new piece of learning is leading.

- Display the learning objective clearly and refer to it regularly throughout the lesson. Explain it in a range of different ways until you are sure all children know what you are aiming to achieve. At different points in the lesson give pupils opportunities to reflect on their progress towards achieving the learning objective.

- Let pupils share how they feel when they have achieved it. Celebrate success! Avoid giving rewards to pupils who achieve the learning objective – develop their intrinsic motivation where the feeling of achievement is reward in itself. Instead reward good behaviour and good listening both of which will help everybody progress.

Agree some success criteria with the pupils and use them

- Enable pupils to reflect on the steps they will need to take to achieve the learning objective.

- Give pupils opportunities to experiment with the learning and then feedback their experiences, both positive and negative. Use these experiences to identify success criteria together. Do not impose your own as these will be less meaningful to the pupils and they may not appreciate the need for each individual step.

- Display the success criteria. Make them accessible to the pupils.

- Model the use of the success criteria for the pupils and check that each criteria is appropriate – they may need to be adjusted.

- Allow pupils time to apply the success criteria in their work.

- Stop at intervals and ask pupils to reflect on their progress. Use techniques such as 'thumbs up' or 'traffic lights' to indicate which success criteria they are fulfilling.

- Ask pupils to underline examples in their work, show a friend or give a suggestion for improvement in their own or others' work.

- Ensure the atmosphere in the classroom is purposeful and active through your own interventions and use of praise when you see pupils meeting each criteria.

- At the end of the lesson identify which elements of the learning were easily achieved or more challenging – these could form future targets.

Focus on questioning

- Look critically at your own questioning style and the range of questions you ask.

- Ask another adult to observe you or make a tape recording.

- Use closed questions to assess knowledge but enable all pupils to respond by asking them to record answers on whiteboards or to show their answer using apparatus or a signal with their hands, or to move to a certain part of the room.

- Ask more open questions where a range of answers is possible so that you enable more pupils to access the learning.

- Be clear why you are asking questions – plan questions that will get to the heart of the new learning.

- Avoid asking superficial questions or getting off the point.

- Use strategies that involve the whole class such as 'Wait Time' when a timer could be used to encourage more pupils to reflect on an answer or ask pupils to close their eyes for thinking time.

- Encourage better quality responses by telling pupils they must use a certain minimum number of words in their answer or use a certain word or words.

- Use talking partners or groups to encourage pupils to come up with extended answers or a number of possible answers.

- Use wrong answers or misconceptions to extend the learning and move everyone forward.

- Treat all answers seriously – if it is not quite what you were looking for, then ask pupils why they have given it or ask others to build on it.

Encourage peer and self-evaluation and peer tutoring

- Give pupils many opportunities to evaluate their own work and that of their peers at all stages in the learning.

- Always evaluate against the agreed success criteria – if, for example, the use of adjectives is the focus of the lesson, then avoid discussing handwriting as it diverts attention away from what matters.

- Let pupils show you their best example or a poor example and give them time to make an improvement.

- Model what good and bad examples are in each different learning context and what improvements could be made.

- Ask them to verbalize how they achieved success, or why they think they found it difficult.

- Encourage them to identify their own strengths and weaknesses and suggest their own areas for improvement.

- Use a marking ladder even with the very youngest in adult-led groups.

- Develop the vocabulary and language of self-evaluation and reflection as early as possible.

- Pair those children who have achieved the learning objective with those who need more support. Encourage them to see that by teaching someone else they are consolidating their own learning and so are more likely to remember it forever – this way everyone benefits.

- Do not underestimate the value of talk.

- Use think starters and prompts to stimulate reflection and thinking; for example, 'I was surprised that…', 'I still wonder about…'.

Child	Marking Ladder for good instructions.	Teacher
	Have you used an inviting opening statement?	
	Have you got an appropriate title?	
	Have you listed the things you need?	
	Are the instructions in the right order?	
	Have you used connectives or numbers for the order?	
	Have you used bossy language? (Verbs)	
	Are your instructions clear?	
	Have you used diagrams or pictures to show what to do?	
	What I did well.	
	What I could improve next time.	

Provide quality feedback

- Give plenty of oral feedback while pupils are on task, asking them regularly to stop and share.

- Assess who is on target with the learning and who needs more support so that you can intervene appropriately.

- Written feedback should focus purely on the learning objective and success criteria. Indicate where there is evidence that the learning objective is being achieved and give concrete suggestions for improvement thereby 'Closing the Gap' between achievement and potential.

- Allow pupils opportunities to make improvements, if not to their own work then to an example that you work through as a group or class.

Adjust your teaching

- Use what you know about pupil progress to adjust what you will do later in the lesson or in the next lesson or series of lessons.

And please keep in touch!

Learning to Learn in Schools is an ongoing Action Research Project. The first two phases demonstrated real gains for the schools taking part in terms of standards of attainment, pupil motivation and teacher morale. The majority of case studies from the first year of Phase 3 found that learning to learn is not only beneficial for pupils in relation to specific aims but also in terms of wider affective outcomes such as increased enthusiasm, motivation and enjoyment in school. To date, the findings are significant enough that the government is listening. Perhaps more importantly you and your colleagues are listening.

As well as our action research, various other learning to learn programmes are developing new insights into teaching and learning (see Section One). Hundreds of teachers throughout the country have taken notice of these developments and started to implement learning to learn in their schools. Learning to learn is by no means an easy fix. It takes thought and planning, and adaptation for the particular school context, but the benefits can be immense both for teachers and for pupils and we are keen to share experience of what works as the approach is developed in schools throughout the UK.

We run a website and a termly e-newsletter so please keep in touch so that you can share your success in putting learning to learn into practice and learn from that of other teachers. Please email your contact details to us at L2L@cflearning.org.uk.

Section Five

Useful resources

Campaign for Learning, Learning to Learn Series

Lucas, B. and Greany, T. (2000) *Learning to learn: setting the agenda for schools in the 21st Century*, Campaign for Learning/Network Educational Press

Lucas, B., Greany, T., Rodd, J. and Wicks, R. (2002) *Teaching pupils how to learn: research, practice and INSET resources*, Campaign for Learning/Network Educational Press

Greany, T. and Rodd, J. (2003) *Creating a learning to learn School*, Campaign for Learning/ Network Educational Press

Section One

Claxton, G. (2004) *Teaching Children to Learn*, National Primary Trust, issue 11

DfES (2003) *Excellence and Enjoyment: A strategy for primary schools*, DfES

DfES (2004a) *Putting People at the Heart of Public Services: Department for Education and Skills five year strategy for children and learners*, DfES

DfES (2004b) *Excellence and Enjoyment: Learning and teaching in the primary years*, DfES, profesional development materials

Hargreaves, D. (2004) *Learning for Life: The foundations for lifelong learning*, Policy Press

Section Two

Black, P., Harrison, C., Lee, C., Marshall, B. and Wiliam, D. (2004) *Working Inside the Black Box: Assessment for Learning in the Classroom*, London: nferNelson

Buzan, T. (2001) *Mind Maps at Work: How to Be the Best at Work and Still Have Time to Play*, London: HarperCollins

Campaign for Learning, www.campaignforlearning.org.uk

Clarke, S. (2001) *Unlocking Formative Assessment: practical strategies for enhancing pupils' learning in the primary classroom*, London: Hodder & Stoughton Educational

Dennison, P. and Dennison, G. (1994) *Brain Gym®: the teacher's edition*, Ventura, CA: Edu-Kinesthetics Inc

Gardner, H. (1993) *Multiple Intelligences*, Philadelphia, PA, Basic Books

Hannan, G. (1991) *Equal Opportunities, Outcomes: Handbooks for Effective Development*, Glasgow: Simon & Schuster Education

Kagan, S. (2001) *Cooperative Learning*, Kagan Publishing: www.kaganonline.com

Mosley, J. (1996) *Quality Circle Time in the Primary Classroom: Your Essential Guide to Enhancing Self-esteem, Self-discipline and Positive Relationships*, Cambridge: LDA, or www.circle-time.co.uk

Smith, A. and Call, N. (1999) *The ALPS Approach – accelerated learning in primary schools*, Stafford: Network Educational Press

University of Newcastle, www.ncl.ac.uk

Section Three

Desforges, C. with Abouchaar, A. (2003) *The impact of parental involvement, parental support and family education on pupil achievement and adjustment: a literature review*, Research Report no 433, DfES

DfES (2003) *Excellence and Enjoyment: A strategy for primary schools*, DfES

DfES (2004a) *Putting people at the heart of public services: Department for Education and Skills five year strategy for children and learners*, DfES

DfES (2004b) *Excellence and enjoyment: learning and teaching in the primary years*, DfES

Hazelbury Infants

Brain Gym®: http://www.braingym.org/

Dennison, P. and Dennison, G. (1994) *Brain Gym®: the teacher's edition*, Ventura, CA: Edu-Kinesthetics Inc

Gardner, H. (1993) *Frames of Mind: Theory of Multiple Intelligences*, Glasgow: Fontana Press

Gardner, H. (1993) *Multiple Intelligences*, Philadelphia, PA: Basic Books

Moseley, J. (1996) *Quality Circle Time in the Primary Classroom: Your Essential Guide to Enhancing Self-esteem, Self-discipline and Positive Relationships*, Cambridge: LDA, or www.circle-time.co.uk

Leaf Lane

Brain Gym®: http://www.braingym.org/

Buzan, T. (2001) *Mind Maps at Work: How to Be the Best at Work and Still Have Time to Play*, London: HarperCollins

Dennison, P. and Dennison, G. (1994) *Brain Gym®: the teacher's edition*, Ventura, CA: Edu-Kinesthetics Inc

Smith, A. (2000) *Accelerated Learning in Practice: Brain-based methods for accelerating motivation and achievement*, Stafford: Network Educational Press

Smith, A. and Call, N. (1999) *The ALPS Approach – accelerated learning in primary schools*, Stafford: Network Educational Press

Smith, A., Lovatt, M. and Wise, D. (2003) *Accelerated Learning: A User's Guide*, Stafford: Network Educational Press

Pennoweth

Buzan, T. (2001) *Mind Maps at Work: How to Be the Best at Work and Still Have Time to Play*, London: HarperCollins

Mosley, J. (1996) *Quality Circle Time in the Primary Classroom: Your Essential Guide to Enhancing Self esteem, Self-discipline and Positive Relationships*, Cambridge: LDA, or www.circle-time.co.uk

St Meriadoc

Black, P., Harrison, C., Lee, C., Marshall, B. and Wiliam, D. (2004) *Working Inside the Black Box: Assessment for Learning in the Classroom*, London: nferNelson

Brain Gym®: http://www.braingym.org/

Buzan, T. (2001) *Mind Maps at Work: How to Be the Best at Work and Still Have Time to Play*, London: HarperCollins

Cam, P. (ed.) (1995) *Thinking Together: Philosophical Enquiry for the Classroom*, The Children's Philosophy Series, Alexandria, NSW: Hale & Iremonger Pty Ltd

CHAMPS®: http://www.learntolearn.org/index_uk.htm

Clarke, S. (2001) *Unlocking Formative Assessment: practical strategies for enhancing pupils' learning in the primary classroom*, London: Hodder & Stoughton Educational

Dennison, P. and Dennison, G. (1994) *Brain Gym®: the teacher's edition*, Ventura, CA: Edu-Kinesthetics Inc

Fisher, R. (1996) *Stories for Thinking*, Nash Pollock Publishing via York Publishing Services

Fisher, R. (1997) *Games for Thinking*, Nash Pollock Publishing via York Publishing Services

Jennings, T. and Philips, G. (2000) *My Little Book of N.L.P: Neuro Linguistic Programming*, ICET

Ready, R. and Burton, K. (2004) *Neuro-Linguistic Programming for Dummies*, Chichester: John Wiley and Sons

St Saviours

Brain Gym®: http://www.braingym.org/

Dennison, P. and Dennison, G. (1994) *Brain Gym®: the teacher's edition*, Ventura, CA: Edu-Kinesthetics Inc

Greenhalgh, P. (2002) *Reaching Out to All Learners: A Mind Friendly Framework for Learning*, Stafford: Network Educational Press

Treloweth

Black, P., Harrison, C., Lee, C., Marshall, B. and Wiliam, D. (2004) *Working Inside the Black Box: Assessment for Learning in the Classroom*, London: nferNelson

Brain Gym®: http://www.braingym.org/

Clarke, S. (2001) *Unlocking Formative Assessment: practical strategies for enhancing pupils' learning in the primary classroom*, London: Hodder & Stoughton Educational

Dennison, P. and Dennison, G. (1994) *Brain Gym®: the teacher's edition*, Ventura, CA: Edu-Kinesthetics Inc

Goleman, D. (1995) *Emotional Intelligence. Why It Can Matter More Than IQ*, London: Bloomsbury

Lawrence, D. (1981) 'The Development of a Self Esteem Questionnaire', *British Journal of Educational Psychology*, 21, 242-221

Mosley, J. (1996) *Quality Circle Time in the Primary Classroom: Your Essential Guide to Enhancing Self esteem, Self-discipline and Positive Relationships*, Cambridge: LDA, or www.circle-time.co.uk

Smith, A. (2000) *Accelerated Learning in Practice: Brain-based methods for accelerating motivation and achievement*, Stafford: Network Educational Press

Smith, A. and Call, N. (1999) *The ALPS Approach – accelerated learning in primary schools*, Stafford: Network Educational Press

Smith, A., Lovatt, M. and Wise, D. (2003) *Accelerated Learning: A User's Guide*, Stafford: Network Educational Press

Wilbury

Clarke, S. (2001) *Unlocking Formative Assessment: practical strategies for enhancing pupils' learning in the primary classroom*, London: Hodder & Stoughton Educational

Section Four

Greany, T. and Rodd, J. (2003) *Creating a learning to learn school*, Campaign for Learning/Network Educational Press

Useful websites

Alite Ltd, www.alite.co.uk

Aspiro, www.aspiroweb.co.uk

BLP, www.buildinglearningpower.co.uk

Campaign for Learning, www.campaignforlearning.org.uk

Department for Education and Skills, www.dfes.gov.uk

Design Council, www.designcounil.org

Jenny Mosley, www.circle-time.co.uk

National College of School Leadership, www.ncsl.org.uk

nferNelson, www.nfer-nelson.co.uk

Teachernet, www.teachernet.gov.uk

Index

Abbreviation: L2L, learning to learn.

achievement, *see* success
action research, 16
activity sheets, for Hazelbury PEPI project, 43–44
Alverton Community Primary School projects, 25–26
analysis of findings, 30
assessment, formative, 95–96, 98–103, 106–114
attainment
    impacts of projects on, 32
        at Leaf Lane, 60
        at St Meriadoc, 83–86
        at St Saviours, 91
        at Treloweth, 101, 102
        at Willbury, 112

badges, 'learning word', 112
Brain Gym®, 88
brain-based learning, handouts for parents, 78–79
Brannel School project, 26
Brettenham Primary School project, 28

Camborne School and Technical College projects, 26–27
Campaign for Learning, 11, 13, 15
    resources, 9–10, 123
celebration of achievement and success, 46–47, 48, 119
children, *see* pupils
Claxton, Guy, quoted, 12–13
Closing the Gap strategies, 109–110
clown puppet PEPI, 45–46
colour groups, 68–70, 73
communication with parents, 41–44
communication skills development, in Hazelbury PEPI project, 38, 39, 40, 45–46, 49
confidence, *see* self-belief and -esteem
creative zone, 67
curriculum limitations, 67

data collection tools, 22
DfES
    quoted, 33
    resources, 13
diaries, learning, 111, 113–114
dyspraxia therapy, 97

Effective Learning Power Profile (ELLI) project, 13, 14
emotional intelligence, 101
evaluation
    by peers, 121
    of L2L projects, 118
evening meetings for parents, 76–81
evidence collection tools, 22

Fallibroome High School project, 24
feedback
    on L2L Action Research project, 122
    on St Meriadoc project, 81–82, 83
    in Treloweth project, 98
5Rs, 18–20
    approaches to, 117–118
    display of, 90, 99
    handouts for parents, 79
Fleecefield Primary School project, 28
    quotations from, 31
formative assessment strategies, 95–96, 98–103, 106–114
Foundation Stage
    Hazelbury PEPI project for, 39, 46
    importance of learning in, 33
    Leaf Lane project for, 53–54
    success criteria in, 101
    teaching stategies for, 53–54

generations of teaching learning, 12–13
goal-setting, in Hazelbury PEPI project, 37
'good learners' handouts, 79
group learning (mixed years), 63–64, 68–70

handouts for parents, 78–79
Hargreaves, David, quoted, 11
Hazelbury Infant School, 35
    PEPI project, 23, 37–50
        quotations from, 48–49
Hazelbury Junior School project, 28
homework, attitudes to, 84–86

John Street Primary School project, 23, 24
    quotations from, 12
Jolly Phonics, 52

Kehelland Village School project, 27
Key Stage 1
    emotional intelligence in, 101
    importance of learning in, 33
    Leaf Lane project for, 54–61
    PEPI project for, 40, 46–47
    teaching stategies for, 52, 54–58

language of L2L, 99, 101, 113–114
Lanner Primary School project, 27
    quotations from, 12, 31
Leaf Lane Infants and Nursery School, 51
    project, 23, 24, 51–61

Learning to learn for life – *research and practical examples for the Foundation Stage and Key Stage 1*

quotations from, 31, 55, 57, 58, 60, 118
learner log books, 56–57, 118
learning diaries, 111, 113–114
learning environment, zoned, 64–66, 73
Learning How to Learn project, 14
learning to learn, 10, 11–12
    characteristics of schools, teachers and pupils,
        116–117
    defining aims for, 116–117
    intervention methods for, 22–23
    need for, 10
    resources, 9–10, 123–124
Learning to Learn Action Research project, 15
    email contact with, 122
    Phases 1 and 2, 16–17, 32
    Phase 3, 17–32
        aims, 18, 21–22
        findings, 30–32
        5Rs framework, 18–20, 117–118
        selection of schools, 17
    resources for projects, 123–125
learning mats, 88, 89–93
learning objectives, 119
Learning Power (in ELLI), 14
learning strategies
    in Hazelbury PEPI project, 38
    in St Saviours project, 93
learning styles, 52, 63, 64, 113
'learning word' badges, 112
learning zones, 64–66
lifelong learning, 11
    5Rs of, 18–20, 117–118
literacy zone, 65
log books, 56 57, 59

marking strategies, 96
meetings for parents, 76 81
Milliband, David, quoted, 13
Mind Maps®, 53, 54–55
mixed year groups, 63–64, 68–70
modelled writing, 106–110
monitoring of L2L projects, 118
motivation
    in Pennoweth project, 63, 71, 73
    in Treloweth project, 99, 101–102
    see also self-motivation

Neuro-Linguistic Programme (NLP), 81
numeracy zone, 65–66

Oakthorpe Primary School project, 29
Ofsted, quoted, 32
organization skills development, in Hazelbury
    PEPI project, 37, 40
Over Hall Community Primary School project,
    24

parents
    benefits of projects for, 32

involvement of, 32, 33
    in Hazelbury PEPI project, 41–44
    in Leaf Lane project, 61
    in St Meriadoc project, 76–86
peer evaluation and tutoring, 121
Pennoweth Community Primary School, 63
    project, 23, 27, 63–73, 118
        quotations from, 71–72, 118
Personal Effectiveness Programme Initiative
    (PEPI), 36, 37–50
planning
    of L2L development, 115–118
    of PI project, 38–40
    of Treloweth project, 98, 101
presentation skills development
    in Hazelbury PEPI project, 40
    to share learning, 59
pupils
    benefits of projects for, 30–31
    L2L characteristics, 117
    responses
        to Pennoweth project, 73
        to St Saviours project, 91–92
        to Treloweth project, 102–103
        to Willbury project, 113
puppetry, in PEPI project, 45–46

QCA schemes, 67
questioning strategies, 120–121
    in Treloweth project, 98

Raynham Primary School project, 29
Readiness, 20
    development
        in Hazelbury PEPI project, 37
        in Pennoweth project, 64
        in St Meriadoc project, 76
        in Treloweth project, 97
recording achievement and success, 46–47, 48,
    119
'recount' lessons, 106–110
reflection wall, 56
Reflectiveness, 20
    development
        in Hazelbury PEPI project, 38
        in Leaf Lane, 51–61
        in Treloweth project, 98
        in Willbury project, 106, 111
    prompts for reflection, 121
    understanding of, 113
Remembering, 20
    development
        in St Saviours project, 89
        in Treloweth project, 98
research skills development, in Hazelbury PEPI
    project, 39, 40
Resilience, 20
    development
        in St Meriadoc project, 76, 83

in St Saviours project, 89
in Treloweth project, 97
Resourcefulness, 20
   development
      in Hazelbury PEPI project, 38
      in Pennoweth project, 63, 64
      in St Saviours project, 89
      in Treloweth project, 97
      in Willbury project, 106
   understanding of, 113
review of L2L projects, 118
Roseland Community School project, 23, 28

St Meriadoc CofE Infant and Nursery School,
   75
   project, 27, 33, 75–86
      quotations from, 32, 83, 84, 86
St Saviours Catholic Infant School, 87
   project, 23, 24, 87–93
      quotations from, 92
SAT results
   at Leaf Lane, 60
   at St Meriadoc, 84–85
   at Willbury, 112
schools
   benefits of projects for, 31–32
   L2L characteristics, 116
secondary schools, learning methods in, 10
self-assessment development, 106
self-belief and -esteem
   development
      in Hazelbury PEPI project, 37
      in St Meriadoc project, 75–76, 83, 86
      in Treloweth project, 101, 102
      in Willbury project, 111
self-esteem, see self-belief and -esteem
self-evaluation skills
   development
      in Leaf Lane project, 55, 56–58
      in Treloweth project, 98, 101
self-evaluation skills development, 119–120,
   121
self-motivation
   development
      in Hazelbury PEPI project, 37
      in Pennoweth project, 64, 67, 71
sharing of learning, 59
speakers at parents' meetings, 80
staff, see teachers
stuckness (being stuck), 90, 92, 97, 99
success, celebration of, 46–47, 48, 119
success criteria, 119–120
   in Treloweth project, 98, 101, 102
   in Willbury project, 106–110, 113
Sutton High School project, 24

teachers
   benefits of projects for, 31
   L2L characteristics of, 116
   responses
      to Hazelbury PEPI project, 52
      to Leaf Lane project, 59, 61
      to Pennoweth project, 71–72
      to St Meriadoc project, 86
      to St Saviours project, 92
      to Treloweth project, 99–102
   training and preparation for L2L, 96, 99–100
teachers' log books, 59
teaching and learning core principles, 34
teaching strategies
   for L2L, 52, 117
      adaptation to progress, 122
   in secondary schools, 10
teamwork for L2L projects, 115–116
thought showers, 111
time management skills development, in
   Hazelbury PEPI project, 39, 40, 42, 48
timetables, in Pennoweth project, 67–70
Treloweth Community Primary School, 95
   project, 28, 95–103
      quotations from, 30, 118

visual, auditory and kinesthetic (VAK)
   communication, 63, 64
vocabulary of L2L, 99, 101, 113–114

Webb, Ann, 119
Willbury Primary School, 105
   project, 29, 105–114
      quotations from, 30, 31
Winsford High Street Community Primary
   School projects, 25
Wolverham Primary School project, 25
Woodford Lodge High School project, 25
working with others
   in Hazelbury PEPI project, 38, 40, 42, 48, 49
   in learning communities, 103
   in peer evaluation and tutoring, 121
   teamwork for L2L projects, 115–116
writing
   improvement
      with formative assessment, 105–114
      with learning mats, 87–88, 89–92

zones of learning, 64–66, 73